The Last Indians
South America's Cultural Heritage

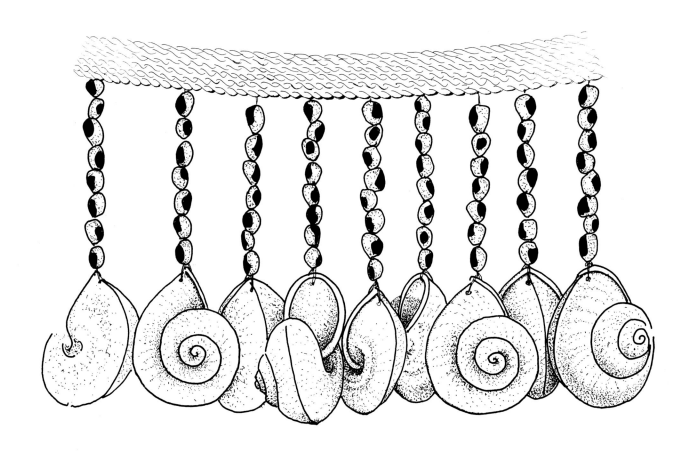

FRITZ TRUPP

The Last Indians
South America's Cultural Heritage

Perlinger

Originally published in German in 1981 under the title 'Die letzten Indianer –
Kulturen Südamerikas' by Perlinger Verlag

© 1981 Fritz Trupp; Perlinger Verlag Ges.m.b.H., Brixentaler Strasse 61,
6300 Wörgl (Austria)
Photography, text and layout: Fritz Trupp
Translation: Christopher Marsh
Drawings: Rudolf Kreuzer
Reproduction: Wagner'sche Univ.-Buchdruckerei, Innsbruck
Produced by Welsermühl, Wels
Printed on Euroart and Euroffset 150 g/m² by PWAG Hallein Papier AG
No part of this publication may be reproduced in whole or in part
without permission in writing from the publisher
ISBN 3-85399-023-1
Printed in Austria

Contents

The South American Indians

500 YEARS AFTER COLUMBUS

October 12, 1492, the day Christopher Columbus, at the age of fifty-one, discovered the Caribbean island of Guanahaní and set foot on the New World, spelled the beginning of the end for many of the indigenous tribes of America.

The Genoese Columbus, who was searching for the Spice Islands, was under the impression he had discovered the sea-route to India. That is why he called the natives 'Indians', a name that subsequent generations have accepted right down to the twentieth century.

Columbus' description of the Indians in his dispatch to the Kind and Queen of Spain, who were backing his expedition, is warmly enthusiastic: "So compliant and peaceful are these people that I can swear to your Majesties that this earth knows no better people. They love their neighbours as themselves; their speech is ever gentle and accompanied by a smile; and although they go naked, yet is their manner seemly and laudable." It is worth pointing out that the great discoverer explicitly referred to the Indians as 'people', an attitude that was not always shared by his successors.

In their dealings with the Indians, the conquerors of America were faced with the kind of difficulty twentieth-century Europeans would have if they were suddenly faced with Martians. In the sixteenth century people just did not know what to make of these beings, how to be-

have towards them, or what was permissible and what was necessary in dealing with them. Above all, the bitter hatred engendered in Europe for the heathen at the time of the crusades against the followers of Islam, for example, did not apply to the Indians; their non-Christian religion did not automatically make them enemies at all. It is true that the white conquerors doubted whether these strange creatures were capable of reasonable thought and were real human beings. And Pope Alexander VI actually had to issue a bull to give official sanction to the view that the natives of America were human beings capable of accepting the Christian faith and to be treated as fellow humans. But this Papal edict did not prevent the Europeans from establishing an efficient system of colonial exploitation. And hand in hand with that, they introduced ethnic barriers, making the colour of a person's skin the key to their system of social and cultural classification.

At the time of the Spanish Conquest America was the home of a huge number of Indian tribes, with different languages and cultures, and different social systems. Thus, the cultural achievements of the Inca, which were in no way inferior to those of contemporary Europe, contrast with the less developed societies of the Indian tribes in the Amazon basin, whose economies featured hunting and wild-plant gathering or horticulture.

In some respects, however, the indigenous peoples were not equal to the Europeans: they had no gunpowder, no horses, no artillery, and they lacked the Europeans' lust for gold and wealth.

Before the white man arrived on the scene, the native population of South America numbered an estimated 50 million. Within only 200 years, this figure was slashed to just over one tenth as disease, forced labour and slavery in the mines and on the sugar-cane plantations all took their toll. The raw materials and wealth of the colonies, meanwhile, were carried away to the Old World, where they helped form the basis for the mercantile system that characterised the European economy in the pre-industrial era.

Among the conquistadors and missionaries, however, there were always a few outstanding individuals willing to defend the human rights of the indigenous American tribes. One of them was the Spanish bishop Bartolomé de las Casas, who threatened to excommunicate anyone who enslaved or mistreated an Indian.

In fact the greatest scourge of the native people was not invading armies or marauding soldiers but the epidemics triggered off by the introduction of wholly new diseases, like measles, smallpox and influenza, to which the Indians had no natural resistance.

Persecution of the Indians stopped only when they had withdrawn high up the mountains, or deep into the jungle, desert or swamp, and their treasures had all been carried away. This phase of relative peace came to an end in the second half of the 19th century when the rubber boom broke out, requiring the availability of cheap labour used to the land and climate. During this period of unlimited economic opportunity, a canoe-load of raw rubber was worth 2500 dollars, and many a trader found himself a millionaire overnight.

Thus 'La Vorágine', a novella written by the Columbian author José Eustasio Rivera, provides a moving account of the sufferings of the Indians at the hands of the rubber farmers. And in 1908 an official commission reported that the British rubber company Peruvian Amazonas Co. had killed about 30,000 Uitoto Indians on its plantations on the Río Putumayo. At that time, it is thought, a ton of rubber was collected at a cost of two human lives. These disclosures led to a wave of protest world-wide, and in Brazil the crimes committed against the Indians triggered off the establishment of the first Indian protection service in South America, the Serviço de Proteção aos Indios (SPI). This organization was headed by Marshal Mariano da Silva Rondon, himself of Indian blood, who created the famous slogan, "Better die than kill an Indian!"

After the end of the rubber boom, the final phase in the conquest of the Indian territories set in. The so-called Indian problem developed into a straightforward land problem when the significance of the vast region of the Amazon basin was suddenly appreciated as a source of mineral wealth, oil, valuable wood, and lush pasture. This led to the arrival of huge farming combines, landless settlers, gold prospectors, and land speculators. For the Indians, the choice quickly became one of withdrawing still further into the jungle or serving their new masters as cheap labour. Those tribes that attempted to resist were either driven off their land or massacred. In 1967 the Brazilian State Department revealed that even the SPI, the Indian Protection Service, had at least been aware of these atrocities and had done nothing to stop them. Consequently, the SPI was dissolved and replaced by the National Indian Foundation in Brazil (FUNAI = Fundação Nacional do Indio).

Reservations to the rescue?

In view of such crimes, various South American governments have since established reservations to protect the indigenous tribes. In Brazil, the brothers Claudio and Orlando Villas Boas deserve great credit for their work in creating a last refuge for more than a dozen small tribal groups, which otherwise would soon have faced extinction. With the support of FUNAI, they set up a protected area on the Río Xingu in the heart of the Mato Grosso, where the various ethnic groups can live their lives according to their own customs and standards, untouched by Christianity or western progress. The reservation itself comprises an area of nearly 6,000 square miles and is closed to all but a few select visitors.

And yet, in the last few years, even this unspoilt paradise has been threatened by a new highway, which now slices through the northern section of the reservation as a feeder road, the BR-80, to the Trans-Amazonica Highway. And in August 1980 a big agricultural combine had a vast expanse of forest cleared, thus reducing still further the territory of the Indians. They, members of the Txukahamai tribe, reacted by attacking the white intruders with their long wooden clubs, causing some fatalities. Subsequently, the Brazilian army had to protect them from a massacre.

This case shows clearly enough that the reservation system can only be successful if the preservation of the tribal lands is seen to be in the interests of the economy and national development. For the small tribal groups in particular, often comprising no more than a few families, it is essential that measures be taken to protect them, to preserve their social and cultural identity. And from this point of view, the much criticised ghetto quality of their existence must be considered the lesser evil.

From jungle to slum

Most researchers and local authorities in South America are convinced that it is a clear case of discrimination not to get the Indians out of the jungle.

Francisco Meirelles, a well-known *sertanista* (which means 'wise in the jungle'), who was given the task of contacting some of the Indian tribes before work started on the Transamazonica, so as to prepare them for the 'dawn of civilisation', put it like this: "Who gives us the right to deprive a certain race of the goods enjoyed by the rest of humanity? Why should human beings continue to pierce their noses and deform their lips, or in general live primitively when they can see a better life? The Indians themselves want to share in the white man's civilisation; they do not want to be museum exhibits for clever people to write books on." (Baumann/Uhlig 1979: 141)

And we cannot ignore the fact that many Indians do want to leave the jungle for the city. It is true that they too are susceptible to the seductions of our technological consumer society. Transistor radios, pink bras, national football heroes, and Condorito, the Latin American version of Micky Mouse, are no longer strangers to the jungle. This change in the life-style of the Indians has usually proved fatal, turning a self-sufficient people into a pool of unskilled and casual labour, with the result that they are growing dependent on other people to give them work and pay their wages so that they can buy things which formerly they either did without or found there for the taking in their natural surroundings. Sometimes they even feel obliged to speak to each other in bad Spanish or Portuguese, because they are ashamed to use their own language in the presence of whites.

Today there is hardly any tribal group that has not had some experience, in one way or another, of the modernisation programmes initiated by the national governments. For the most part, the increase in civilisation has not been accompanied by a similar increase in culture or in the general quality of life.

Some autochthonal groups, however, have managed remarkably well to adapt to these new conditions and yet preserve their identity. There are many Indian tribes with the spiritual strength to accept those gifts of civilisation that they find useful, while rejecting those they see are a threat to their survival as a group.

For many years the solution to the Indian problem was thought to lie in keeping the Indian tribes in governmental, religious and scientific leading-strings, a situation that became particularly disturbing when they were subjected to attempts to force political, missionary or commercial interests on them without being permitted to form their own judgment. It took a long time until it was realised that the Indians ought to be allowed to determine their own fate. A crass example of alien influence is to be found in many of the wide variety of missionary groups, including the sect which achieved notoriety a few years ago through the mass suicide of its members in Guyana.

Bartomeu Melia, a Jesuit priest and former co-ordinator of the Catholic Church's Indian policies in Paraguay, is one man who is aware of the problems of missionary work directed at the Indians. In the magazine 'Pogrom', he wrote the following: "There are some Christian missionary movements that come to the Indians and try to 'convert' them without being able to judge or knowing anything about the Indians' own religious values. Such missionaries forget that robbing Indians of the religious convictions that form the very foundation of their philosophy and of their human relationships is to deprive them of their identity and split their personalities. Yet there is no need to manufacture a heathen just to get a Christian."

In the last few years, however, there have been signs of a new approach, especially within the Catholic orders. This new attitude to Indian cultures is reflected in the support given to Indian autonomy campaigns. Thus, with the aid of the Salesians, the Federación Shuar in Ecuador has developed into the most important Indian movement in Latin America.

At the same time, the Indians themselves seem to be developing a greater ethnic consciousness in many South American countries, and there are signs of a development there similar to the growth of the 'Red Power' movement in North America. Demographically, too, the Latin American Indians are showing a newly found vitality, with their numbers increasing everywhere.

Who is an Indian?

Nowadays the term 'Indian' denotes not so much the racial characteristics as the socio-economic situation of an ethnic group. The word 'Indio', which sounds harmless enough to us, has in fact taken on a perjorative meaning like that of the English word 'nigger'. For this reason the terms 'indígena' and 'pueblos indígenas' (indigenous peoples) are now official terminology in South America.

In fact after 400 years of intermarriage, the population can no longer be classified on the basis of purely racial criteria. Often it is not even clear where to draw the line; and opinions differ on how to establish membership of the aboriginal Indian societies. So the question, "Who is an Indian?" is frequently treated in linguistic or cultural terms and answered on the basis of the language in domestic use or the type of clothing worn. Nevertheless, it is important to distinguish between the highland Indians, that is the descendants of the old civilisations of the Andean regions, and the lowland Indians, comprising a huge number of small tribes located primarily in the Amazon basin. Even the term 'tribe' is sometimes problematical, because these groups often lack a supreme political authority.

The Indian peoples of South America have much in common. But the differences are no less numerous. The number of Indian languages, for example, is estimated at over 500, some of them as dissimilar as English and Chinese. While some of these languages, like Quechua and Aymara in the Andean states, are spoken by several million people, others, like the Záparo language found in the jungle of Ecuador, are spoken by no more than a few individuals.

The number of lowland Indians in South America is put at about a million. That is very little considering that the indigenous tribes inhabit a vast area that extends from the Caribbean coast in the north to the Gran Chaco in Paraguay and includes the jungles of the Orinoco and Amazon basins. That latter alone extends over a distance equal to that between London and Moscow or Los Angeles and Florida. After almost 500 years of colonial or national rule, only very few tribal groups have succeeded in withdrawing far enough or adapting skilfully enough to escape cultural annihilation. And yet there are still grounds for hope, as the examples in this book show, that various Indian peoples will manage to nurture their identity with new developments from a fading culture and thus escape the vortex of anonymity generated by pseudo-civilisation.

The 'last' of the Indians, who have preserved the cultural heritage of their forefathers, need not be ashamed of their so-called backwardness: Their contributions to natural science and botany are a valuable addition to the sum total of the human knowledge of modern man. At a time when technological progress is viewed as a potential threat in many fields of our own lives, the values embodied in the Indian cultures of South America can provide a healthy stimulus to reconsider the life-style of today's industrial society, particularly social principles that base on partnership, not privilege, or ecological principles that base on co-existence, not destruction.

Or, in the words of the shaman of the Juruna Indians: "One day, when there are no trees left, the heavens will fall and all men be destroyed."

The Yanomami

Until recently the Yanomami Indians, who inhabit the border regions of Venezuela and Brazil, were considered to be the last Indians untouched by civilisation on the whole subcontinent of South America. For centuries their reputation as fiercesome warriors and the inaccessibility of their homelands had enabled them to live their lives undisturbed and to preserve their culture to a very great extent. Moreover, the government has imposed strict laws which exclude all but a few research workers from the tribal areas.

The territory inhabited by the Yanomami is approximately the size of Austria. In Venezuela it comprises the upper Orinoco basin and the rivers Mavaca, Ocamo, Putaco and Siapa. The Sierra Parima, at 1000 metres the watershed between the Orinoco and Amazon, forms the border between Venezuela and Brazil and the heart of the Yanomami territories. On the Brazilian side, the Yanomami are found along the rivers Uraricuera, Catrimani and Dimini.

In the last few years, however, the situation of these Indians has also started to change with the discovery of uranium and other mineral deposits, and the introduction of development projects. Thus the Brazilian authorities are planning to build a road through the jungle from Manaus to Caracarai, which will pass through the tribal territories of the Yanomami. Already a large number of Indians have died of the diseases introduced by prospectors and workers, including tuberculosis, influenza and measles. Considerable alarm was caused by an epidemic of another new disease to the area, namely onchocercosis, a worm infection transmitted by black-fly that can lead to blindness. Some time ago the Brazilian National Indian Foundation (FUNAI) therefore decided to establish a reservation for the Yanomami. But since then nothing has been done to implement the plan.

The Yanomami, whose name in their own language means 'man', can be divided into a number of subgroups: the Shamatari, Waika, Sanemá, Shirishana and Guajahibo. An estimated 15 to 25,000 live in Venezuela, while their number in Brazil is put at about 10,000. The majority of linguists presume that theirs is an isolated language totally unrelated to any other.

Interestingly enough, it is the Yanomami, who only started to take a sporadic interest in horticulture about a hundred years ago and have therefore been a tribe of hunters and gatherers for most of their history, who now represent the numerically strongest group of jungle Indians in South America. But today game is very scarce, and they now grow plantain and gather the fruit of the pijiguao palm as the basis of both their economy and their diet. Increased contact with missions and the local mestizo population has also ushered in cultural change in many respects. And whereas the Yanomami formerly lived mainly along the minor tributaries in the deepest jungle, they now tend to settle on the Orinoco for easier access to western consumer goods.

On the interface with civilisation the outward tokens of this new life-style are already to be seen: European dress, houses built on mestizo lines, an outboard for the dugout as part of the government's development programme, and the profane use of ritual appurtenances. One example of the latter is the use of drugs, which traditionalist Indians accept only in a ceremonial context but which has degenerated in some places under the influence of an alien culture into a pure stimulant or compensation mechanism.

War and peace

The Indians with their six-foot-long bows make a truly anachronistic impression as they wait to greet a representative of western civilisation as he touches down on a jungle landing strip, with the skyscrapers of Caracas only two and a half hours away by air.

And yet, despite their many contacts with the outside world, the Yanomami have retained their traditional martial attitude and their ideal of the courageous warrior. And conflicts are common enough in a setting of constant blood feuds triggered off by wife-snatching, black magic, murder and theft.

But before the men plan an attack, they first assemble with their bows and arrows, and now sometimes with their rifles, too, to sing their war song: "I, the vulture, am hungry for flesh!"

When he started his work with the Yanomami, by whom he was highly esteemed, the Salesian missionary, the late Padre Cocco is said to have tried to pacify the warlike tribe. To this end he arrived with a plane-load of presents, which he exchanged for the Indians' bows and arrows, which he then sold to the souvenir dealers in Caracas. With the proceeds he then purchased another load of presents and flew back to the jungle to collect still more weapons. Unfortunately, Padre Cocco's laudable plan was foiled by the cunning of the Yanomami, who simply restocked their arsenal between each flight.

But the Yanomami also perform ritual duels as a more sporting way of settling their differences or working off their aggressions. They may take the form of boxing matches, with the fighters aiming at their opponents' loins and chest, while a duel with huge wooden clubs is a more ferocious affair, that often enough finishes up with broken heads and bones. The fighters take turns at aiming a blow at their opponents' skulls. Should one collapse after the first blow, his brother is entitled to reciprocate and thus end the duel.

The first authentic report on the life-style of the Yanomami was by Helena Valero, who was carried off by the Indians as a young girl and lived with them for twenty years. Now she lives on the upper Orinoco with her sons, whose bilingualism makes them natural go-betweens for whites and the Yanomami.

Ettore Biocca, an Italian anthropologist, has since published her life-story, presenting a clear picture of the conflicts and disputes, and also of the ill-treatment meted out to the Yanomami women as a consequence of the tribe's masculine ethos of the fearless warrior. On the other hand, it is worth pointing out that the Yanomami's aggression and their forays involve few fatalities. Nor do they reach the degree of violence that can be witnessed in our cities every day.

The Yanomami Indians live in about 150 villages, called *shabonos*, which form independent social units. Each village community lays claim to its own territory, which it needs for hunting and also, on the *conucos* (plantations), for farming.

The Yanomami possess very few household effects, and they are designed solely for the needs of man in the rain forest. Their most important piece of 'furniture' is the hammock, an invention that represents one of the great cultural achievements of the lowland Indians. Every family has its own fireplace, and their domestic utensils comprise woven bowls, baskets and gourds, plus aluminium pans acquired from the missions through barter.

No use for clothes

Male dress consists of a string tied around the hips and fastened to the foreskin to hold the penis upright. On ceremonial occasions their upper arms and shoulders are decorated with colourful feathers. The women also go naked and wear a string around their waists, to which various small items can be fastened. They place flowers and thin rods through their pierced ears and nasal septum. Both male and female wear their hair in the form of a tonsure reminiscent of medieval monks. Sometimes this reveals the scars the men have received in their duels.

In general, natural ornament takes the place of clothing, or, as the Indians put it, "Body paint is our second skin." Their red paint is derived from the seminal capsules of the onoto shrub, violet from the fruit of a palm, and black, the colour of war and death, from soot and ashes. The applied motifs have not just an aesthetic function; they are a part of their magic and religious traditions.

Dream world of the soul

Tribal traditions are preserved and handed down by the shamans, who are skilled in all the rites of the tribe. The Yanomami call them *shaboliwa*. With the help of drugs these men, for men they must be, are able to penetrate into other worlds, which are closed to ordinary mortals. They are believed to unite with the *hekura*, the spirits of the jungle and its animals, and with the natural elements, a metamorphosis that can only be achieved under the influence of drugs. For this purpose they make use of various hallucinogens taken in the form of snuff.

The most common is called *yopo* or *ebena* and is derived from the tree *Anadenatha peregrina*. The seminal capsules of the tree are dried, crushed to a powder and

17 Our arrival in the village is observed by a suspicious warrior of the Iyëwei-teri.

18/19 Traditional Yanomami architecture is still to be found at the headwaters of the Orinoco. The individual families live under a continuous ring of sloping windscreens surrounding a large open space. This aboriginal form of village architecture blends harmoniously into the jungle environment.

20 Bow and arrows are always ready to hand. The bows are six feet long and made of ironwood. A number of different arrowheads are used.

21 For water transport, the Wabutawë-teri make use of a large piece of bark. This archaic bark boat can only be used to travel with the current. Today the Yanomami have almost entirely adopted the dugouts of their neighbours.

22/23 A tug of war in the Kashorawë-teri *shabono.* The Indians are thought to have played this popular game before the arrival of the white man.

24/25 Taking *ebena* snuff. The two men use a tube to blow the hallucinogenic powder up each other's nostrils. Soon afterwards they experience visions and go into an ecstatic trance.
Bottom left: Under the influence of drugs a shaman imitates the spirit of a jaguar.

mixed with the ash of the bark of *Elisabetha princeps.*

Another important substance for making *yopo* is taken from the inner cortical layer of the tree *Virola elongata,* which is mixed with other vegetable ingredients.

The Yanomami males consume large amounts of *ebena* every day. To take the drug, two men use a long smooth tube to blow it up each other's nostrils in several small doses.

The effect of this hallucinogenic snuff quickly wears off, so that further doses must soon be taken. The drug users can be identified by the increased secretion of nasal mucous, their apathetic expression and twitching muscles.

Once their visions have started, the shamans begin to dance back and forth with their arms raised, singing a melodious song. This is to invoke their tutelary spirits to enter into their breasts. Others kneel on the ground and imitate the mythical beasts they are turning into. Only when they have fallen into a trance can the *shaboliwa* travel through the cosmos, protecting the community from danger, and diagnosing and healing illness.

The principal therapy available to the shaman in his role as healer is to suck the disease, which is thought to have material form, out of the patient's body.

Shamanism, in one form or another, is a worldwide phenomenon. Many scholars

26/27 The mourning rites of the Iyëwei-teri. With an air of great solemnity, the assembled relatives drink the mixture of puréed plantain and the ashes of the deceased. This ritual ceremony guarantees that the strength of the deceased is transferred to the village community.

28/29 The black face paint can symbolise either sorrow or war. The white down feathers are also visible in the dark and indicate the visitors' peaceful intentions.

30/31 Mist forest.

32 The dynamic unity formed by body, bow and arrow. The hunter tries to kill a turtle with an indirect shot.

33

believe its origins go back over 50,000 years to Siberia, from where it spread to America with the first immigrants. The aspect of shamanism that distinguishes the shamans from the medicine-men is the ecstatic trance and the migration of the soul.

A shaman is normally selected for office by supernatural beings and must undergo an initiation phase, rather like an apprenticeship, in order to acquire his paranormal powers. His most important function is that of healer, and as such he makes use of the earliest forms of medical techniques. So far there is no scientific explanation for the success achieved by many shamans in treating their patients. In some cases the placebo effect may play a role, with the patient basically curing himself of his ailment through his own belief in a cure.

Some psychologists have described the shaman as having a soul with a primeval structure, from which all our dreams and hallucinations derive. In this dream world of the soul, man no longer feels himself to the distinct from his environment but rather to form part of a collective of trees, rivers, mountains, animals and plants. In this context C. G. Jung speaks of the archetypes that constitute part of the collective unconscious in man. And this would explain the many similarities in mythology and in the religious ideas of shamanism.

Mourning rites

One of the most important events in the lives of the Yanomami Indians is a ceremony that is held in honour of the dead. When a Yanomami dies, his body is cremated, and the remaining bones are crushed to a powder by his relatives and then stored in a gourd. Once a year, the anniversary of his death is observed in the form of a ceremony during which the remains of the deceased are mixed with puréed plantain and drunk by the members of his family. Only then, the Yanomami believe, will the soul of the deceased be free and enter into the life beyond. Such rites are referred to as endocannibalism by the ethnologists.

In the village of the Iyewei-teri I once had an opportunity to witness such a ceremony. For several days previously the men had been out hunting in order to be able to entertain the invited guests. The mourning rites were being observed for a woman who had died of an arrow wound received in hostilities with another group of Yanomami. It was quite impossible to discover who the victim was, however, as it is completely taboo for the Yanomami to reveal a person's name.

Particular significance is attached to the welcoming ceremony for the invited guests, with whom alliances are often made and presents exchanged. The official conversation begins in the form of a

34

ritual recitative, known as *pedir coroto* in the *lengua geral*. The Yanomami call it *waya mou*, which simply means 'asking for presents'. For this part of the ritual several pairs of men stand facing each other at the centre of the village, each with a bundle of bows and arrows in his hand, and discuss the latest news and the items they hope to barter in the form of antiphonal song. This is accompanied by rhythmic motions, while the partners reiterate their standpoints in formal dialogue. My interpreter, Manuel Valero, translated one of these ceremonial dialogues for me:

"My patience will soon be exhausted. I have come here as a friend, and now I shall speak. I want you to give me much *coroto*. You are always getting presents. Sister Maria at the mission and the doctor at the malaria clinic give you aluminium pans, fishing hooks and a lot of medicines. We have nothing, because they give us nothing. It is time I got a machete. Last week the Bisaasi-teri took one of our girls. So we broke one of their arms with a cudgel. If you don't give me a machete, I shall turn nasty soon!"

These dialogues last until the following morning, when the puréed plantain with the ashes of the deceased is drunk by everyone to the accompaniment of loud wailing and moaning.

During the ceremony I noticed one particularly striking group of males. Their

faces were painted black, which is the symbol of death. After the presents had been handed out, they took their weapons and silently left the village. The next act of the feud had begun.

The Yanomami believe that man has more than one soul, although the idea of the soul in the sense of our western civilization is in any case misleading when applied to the religious beliefs of the Indians. According to Zerries and Schuster (1974), *nobolebe*, the soul of the deceased, ascends into the heavens with the smoke of the funeral pyre, where it unites with *noneshi*, the shadow soul. Every person has a shadow soul, that is a kind of *doppelgänger* in the form of a small being who settles either in the person himself or in an animal or plant. This motif of an *alter ego* is very common among the Indian tribes of America. In the case of men, *noneshi* prefers to reside in the harpy-eagle, black-face monkey or jaguar, depending on the person's mythological kinship. A woman's shadow soul is said to dwell within the otter. If an animal that houses a *noneshi* dies, the person to whom the shadow soul belongs dies too. A third category of soul is that of the image soul, or *noudibe,* which is especially attributed to children.

There is no danger, however, that a hunter might inadvertently commit suicide by slaying the animal that houses his own shadow soul, as the animal bearing a person's *noneshi* always avoids that person.

Children who lose their shadow soul are at particular risk and fall ill. In such an event all the members of the *shabono* start a search in order to find the soul and bring it back. Here, too, the shaman, under the influence of drugs, plays a major role, entreating his tutelary spirits to bring back the shadow soul.

When the Yanomami die, their souls pass through the various levels of the cosmic universe until they reach a heavenly crossroads. There they are separated by a judge of souls. Those who always shared their possessions with others are sent to a kind of paradise where everyone is young and the pijiguao palm always bears fruit. The warriors who fell in battle are sent to a pile-village that also exists in heaven. And only those who were miserly on earth are dispatched to hell's fire, where they must endure death for ever and ever.

37 A light-skinned Kashorawë-teri girl is painted with *onoto* in readiness for a celebration. The dye consists of the seeds of *Bixa orellana* mixed with a palm oil to form a paste.

38/39 The aesthetic feeling of the Yanomami is expressed primarily in the carefully executed body and face paintings. The motifs used are either a part of their magico-religious tradition or an expression of personal experiences. Eighty different patterns for face painting have been recorded to date.

40 Even small girls are decked out in face paint and thin rods that are passed through the nasal septum, lower lip and the corners of the mouth.

41 The children are free to romp and play by the river. The affection the Yanomami lavish on their children does not bear out the cliché of the 'wild ways' of the Yanomami. And children crying is a rare sound in the *shabono.*

42/43 Trials of strength provide an outlet for pent-up emotions or aggression.

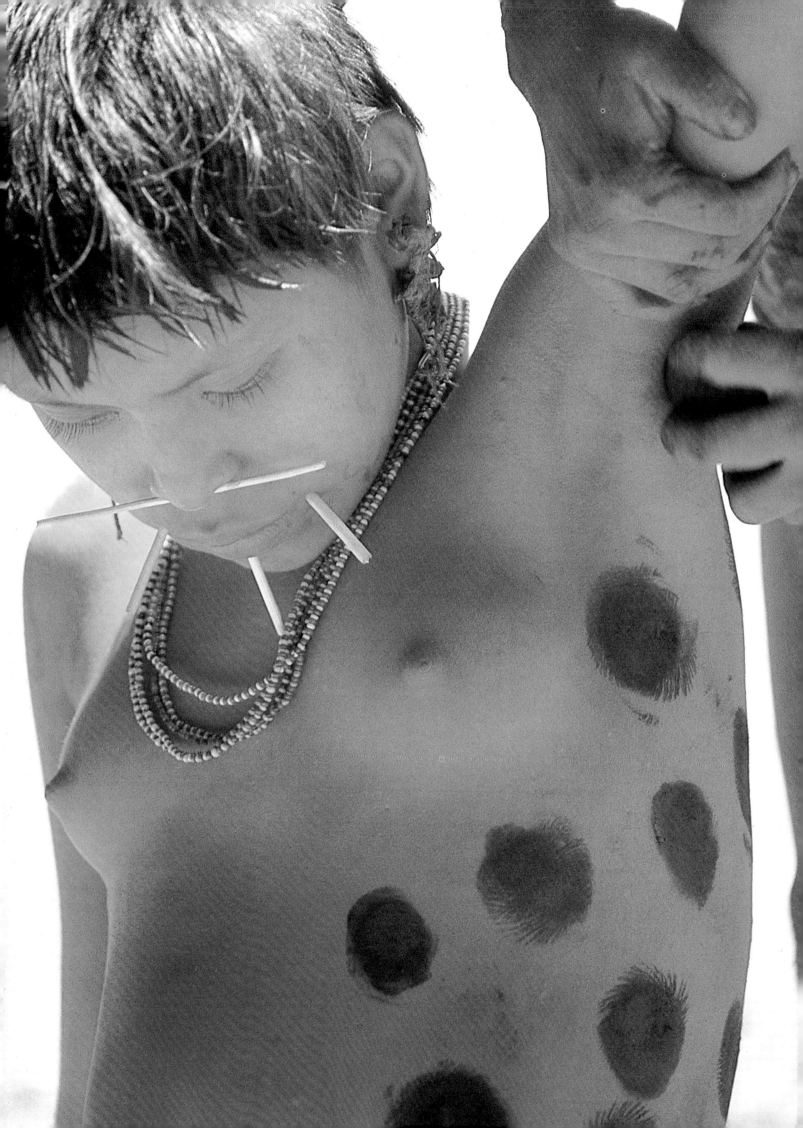

The Cuna

The Comarca de San Blas is an archipelago, 125 miles long and 12 miles wide, lying off the Caribbean coast of Panama. The group of islands is inhabited by the Cuna Indians, who have been more successful in preserving their own culture than just about any other ethnic group in America.

San Blas has not always been the home of the Cuna. They originally inhabited the jungles of Darien, the isthmus between South and Central America, where they were disturbed by the Spanish Conquistadors. The cruelty of their new masters as well as the missionary activities of the Church triggered off a general migration to the Atlantic coast, from where they fought a bitter guerilla war against the Spaniards. But their relationship with the English and French pirates who made the waters of the Caribbean unsafe in the 18th century was quite friendly. The pirates frequently used the Cuna settlements as a base, and sometimes the Cuna participated in joint forays.

Contacts with Europeans intensified in the 17th century. According to the English chronicler Waffer, 1200 Scottish settlers arrived in Darien and were given a friendly reception by the natives. And even though the settlers were soon expelled again by the Spaniards, they left their mark on the Indian culture there, as the dress of the Cuna women clearly shows.

The San Blas Islands themselves were not settled until the 19th century, and there were a number of causes for this migration, such as the Cuna Indians' poor relationship with the Creoles and Negroes on the mainland, the mosquito problem on the coast, and the increasing significance of the coconut trade. But a number of Cuna Indians are still to be found on the mainland today, living along the border between Panama and Colombia.

After the foundation of the Republic of Panama, the new government tried to force the Cuna Indians to change their life-style. In the twenties, several police stations were built on the archipelago, the women were forbidden to wear their traditional dress, and the sacred effigies of the spirits were taken from the medicine-men and burnt. And that was the signal for the last Indian rebellion in

The men gather in an assembly house for a ritual smoke (Waffer 1699). Today the Cuna men all wear western clothes.

Latin America. In 1925 the Cuna launched a swift and sure attack, occupying the government offices, killing a few policemen and finally expelling the interlopers. A group of commandos sent to counterattack by the Panamanian government was prevented from reaching San Blas by the appearance of an American cruiser from the Canal Zone. Ever since then the Cuna have enjoyed a considerable degree of autonomy on San Blas, which was made into an independent reservation.

The success of their revolt, the pressures from without and also their isolated loca-tion, all helped forge a political unit out of what had previously been a hopelessly divided people. Moreover, the democratic structure of their society is pretty much unique in the Third World. This applies particularly to their *congreso*, around which their political life revolves. This is a kind of parliament, to which all the adult males of an island belong. It is accommodated in a separate assembly house, where the men meet every day to discuss unsolved problems and unresolved disputes, before making a joint decision. The actual head of the social hierarchy of the Cuna is the *saila* or village chief, who, like all officers, is elected by the male population. For every aspect of local life the community elects a separate officer, including one for housing and one for the coconut plantations, while the Cuna also maintain their own 'police force' to preserve law and order.

Today there are about 20,000 Cuna living on 50 of the 400 islands of San Blas. Several of these islands are no bigger than a football pitch and have been enlarged by tipping refuse, and sand and stone from the mainland onto the coral banks. Cuna houses, which are rectangular on plan, are built of palm wood and split sugarcanes, with a roof of leaves. The villages themselves are all located near the coast, because drinking water and agricultural products have to be transported from the mainland. Their own crops primarily comprise sugar-cane, plantain, manioc, cacao, pepper and tobacco. The coconut plantations, their most important source of revenue, are situated on the more remote islands. To supplement their income, the Cuna also fish and hunt turtle. They are excellent sailors in their dugouts driven by sail or an outboard.

Formerly, many Cuna men were to be found among the crews of European and

A village street on San Blas. The walls of the houses and the fences for the patio are made of tightly packed canes, which have to be specially transported to the islands by boat.

American ships, but today they prefer to seek work for a few years in Panama City or the Canal Zone. When they return to the islands, they have to pay a kind of tax to the village community as compensation for the local services they have not rendered during their absence.

Molas and gold

Mola is the name of the extremely beautiful traditional dress of the Cuna women, which has become an unofficial symbol of Panama. These *molas* are a creation of the Cuna women themselves, which they have developed from European models. In the 19th century the women wore a kind of chemise with a red band at the hem, which grew wider and wider in the course of the years. Then at the beginning of the 20th century, Panamanian traders introduced flowing wrap-around skirts, and the Cuna women transferred their patterns, which are done in appliqué work, to the top. The motifs they use can be abstract or they can have animal or human form, and often they represent scenes from Indian mythology. Appliqué work with multi-coloured layers of material is a complicated technique that requires both patience and great skill. The various layers of carefully cut cotton fabric, dyed in all different colours, are placed on top of each other and sewn to-

44 Cuna girl with splendid gold ornaments from the Island of Nalunega.

49 Coconuts are the most important item of trade on the archipelago of San Blas.

50/51 Coconut palms and Indian houses in close proximity. Many islands are so small that they had to be enlarged by tipping rock and earth.

52 Water is precious on San Blas. It has to be transported in gourds from the mainland.

53 Thanks to their dug-outs or *cayucos,* the Cuna are able to maintain fields on the mainland as well.

54 A young woman in everyday dress. The first European invaders were also highly impressed by the splendour of their gold jewellery. Today the Cuna acquire their breast plates, ear-rings and nose rings from jewellers in Panama or Colombia.

55 Top: The gold rings worn by the Cuna women on every finger are a status symbol.
Bottom: The women make colourful arm and leg bands, often with fancy patterns, out of imported beads called *wini.*

56 Crushing the rice.

gether in such a way that the pattern of the underlying fabric remains visible through the top layer.

Today the richly decorated blouses of the Cuna women are a real mine of information for the anthropologist, as the designs reflect the cultural influences and changes in the lives of the Cuna tribe. The old *molas* from the turn of the century are particularly sought after, because the motifs, which have a marked symbolic character, are no longer in use now.

Another striking aspect of the Cuna women is their gold jewellery. A 17th century historian wrote that a woman was considered poor if she wore less than 15 or 20 pounds of gold. In the meantime the Cuna have stopped making their own jewellery. They now buy it from dealers, although the old motifs have largely been retained. And gold is still worn in everyday life by the Cuna women and has a high status value.

Medicine-men

The Cuna Indians have a particular respect for their religious concepts and ritual and for their traditional mythology. One of the central figures in their mythology is Ibeorkun, who taught man how to live his life.

The mediators between ordinary mortals and such supernatural beings are members of the tribe who are thought to have special abilities and magical powers.

Thus every village has at least one *innatuledi,* a kind of medicine-man. This medicine-man must first serve a one-year apprenticeship with an old master, who teaches him the ceremonial songs and the nature of the medicinal herbs. On some islands there are actual schools where acknowledged medicine-men provide tuition for aspirants to the office.

The healing process focusses on the ritual incantation of magic formulas. These songs are actually written down in a form of hieroglyphics, with a separate symbol used for every herb and for every magic invocation, which serves as a mnemonic for the *innatuledi,* who copies them into his note-box in pencil or crayon. These symbols can only be read by a certain group of medicine-men, as every 'school' has its own system of symbols. The function of this pictographic record is not so much to preserve the individual concepts as to maintain the correct sequence of the incantations.

According to the spiritual beliefs of the Cuna Indians, a man falls ill because his *purba,* a kind of soul, has been carried away by evil spirits. But that is not man's only soul; he also has *tula,* the life force, and *niga,* without which he cannot exist. And a fourth soul is *kurgin,* a magic force from which a person derives his individual talent.

Wooden figures with inner life

Purba ist not limited to man alone; it is also present in plants and animals. Even the *uchu,* the wooden figurines of the Cuna, possess a *purba,* and the medicine-man can ask the *purba* of an *uchu* to help him recover the abducted soul. His tutelary spirits then enter the underworld, where they fight with the evil powers in the *kalu,* or caves, for the possession of the patient's soul.

The *uchu* are 10 to 45 centimetres high and dressed in European attire. Very few of them have the features of an Indian. It is believed that these figurines are a product of contact with Europeans and the subsequent introduction of the steel axe and other tools in the last few centuries. The wooden statues themselves have no name but rather are known by the name of the wood from which they are carved. This is because their significance lies not in their external features but in the power

of the *purba* residing in the tree involved. For the healing ceremony itself, the various *uchu* are stood under the patient lying in his hammock. The medicine-man holds in his hand a carved stick, which he uses to summon the spirits, and he also has a kind of censer in which he burns cocoa beans and tobacco to produce a smell the *uchu* like.

The Cuna also have another group of holy men, called *nele,* who are born with magic powers. These powers are the gift of Ibeorkun and must be developed through training. The *nele* can see into the future and converse with the spirits in their dreams. In cases of serious illness, the Indians go to the *nele,* who enjoys the highest esteem in Cuna society. His contacts with the world of the spirits permit him to make the diagnosis and prescribe the appropriate medicine.

The actual therapy, however, is the task of the *innatuledi,* who must also gather the curative herbs and assemble the paraphernalia of his art. The services of the medicine-man are paid in cash, the price depending on the length of the treatment.

Large gatherings with shamanistic character are also a part of Cuna life, such as the puberty ceremonies for girls, the consecration of a new assembly hall, or the ritual performed at the outbreak of an epidemic. In such cases the spiritist leader of the Cuna is the *absogedi.*

Today the Cuna carve dolls of balsa-wood to sell to the tourists. They are complete with typical Cuna female dress.
Left: A child plays with a 'ghost boat' made of balsa, which accompanies the souls of the dead into the hereafter. The boat is crewed by two *uchu* figurines on the deck.

In the summer of 1980 an Ina festival was held on the island of Nalunega for a group of girls who had reached sexual maturity. For this puberty ceremony the girls had their hair cut short for the first time in their lives. The *absogedi* had instructed every family to carve one male and one female figure out of balsa. For the ceremony, more than fifty almost life-size cylindrical *nia* figures were stood in the assembly hall. Their function is to restrain the evil spirits, the *poni*, that are threatening the girls. The *absogedi* summoned the *purba* of his tutelary spirits, who thereupon entered into the *nia* figures so as to keep the girls out of the clutches of the demons. After the ceremony the spirit souls depart, and the wooden statues lose all magical significance. The Indians stand them in their garden or throw them into the sea.

An indication of the strength of Cuna belief in their traditional rites is the fact that a sacred *uchu* statue is not to be had at any price. The sale of a statue would arouse the wrath of the spirits, who would bring disease and disaster upon the Indians. Thanks to their loyalty to their traditions, and their ability to seek solutions to problems arising from contact with modern industrial society, the Cuna have managed to preserve their cultural identity to this very day.

Today, the tropical beauty of the San Blas Islands and the exotic character of their

61 The dark-blue line painted on the bridge of this old woman's nose is a protection against the *poni* or evil sprits.

62 Top: A medicine-man or *innatuledi* invokes the spirits. For this purpose he burns cacao seed in a clay censer and smokes a pipe. The smell attracts his tutelary spirits, which thereupon enter into the wooden figurines or *uchu*.
Bottom: Magic wood carvings are just as much a part of the paraphernalia of the medicine-man as his roots and medicinal herbs.

63 During the puberty celebrations, the girls are protected from the *poni*, the evil spirits, by life-size *nia* figures.

64 Top: The *uchu* are stored in a wooden box. Their function is to help the medicine-man recover the souls that have been carried off to the underworld.
Bottom: Cuna pictography. The various signs represent certain medicinal herbs.

65 Other pictograms have a mythological significance, such as the journey of the soul to the *kalu*, the caves of the underworld.

66 The *uchu* are always dressed western-style. These statues derive their significance not from their outer shape but from the wood of which they are carved.

67 The figurines of the spirits are given a bath daily to keep them happy.

68 Two appliqué motifs from a *mola*, with a tree of life as the central motif and below that a mythological bird.

inhabitants are being efficiently marketed as a tourist attraction by the big tour operators. On one or two of the islands there are now landing strips and simple hotels, although most tourists arrive in light aircraft and fly back to Panama the same day. Many visitors get the impression of being in one vast ethnographic museum. This feeling of unreality comes to an abrupt end when they take their first photograph – and have to pay. Some of them complain of what they see as the avarice of the Cuna. But the 'unpolished' way the tourists are sometimes treated is simply the Cuna Indians' defence against importunate visitors and over-eager photographers. In fact, no tourist is allowed to spend the night on an island that is inhabited by Indians. And it is not the Indians on San Blas who are living in a ghetto but the visitors. The Cuna have thus been largely successful in protecting themselves from excessive cultural pressures from the outside world, unlike many other exotic tourist destinations in other tribal areas, where the impact of tourism has had a detrimental effect from the ethnological point of view.

A *cazique* with his wife and servants (Waffer 1699).

Ghosts of Granite

ANCIENT INDIAN ROCK-ART IN NORTH-WEST AMAZONIA

Rock or cave paintings and carvings are to be found in every continent of the world, but the specimens that have been discovered throughout the whole of South America pose some intriguing questions on the prehistory of the subcontinent. Often these works are of an artistic standard that would do credit to any modern artist. They display a variety of styles, which one might classify in western terms as abstract or naturalistic but are very difficult to interpret through western eyes. Many of the findings in South America are excellent examples of the so-called 'x-ray style', which is also found throughout the world. In such works the animal-like or anthropoid creatures are depicted in outline combined with internal bodily organs as in an x-ray.

In many cases it has not been possible to date these rock-paintings and engravings. A comparison on the basis of style or technique with sites in Europe, Africa or Australia is not meaningful in view of the total absence of any chronological correlation between them. In Europe the paleolithic cave-paintings go back 10,000 to 25,000 years, whereas those found in Australia are only a few centuries old. Since the subcontinent of South America was first settled over 20,000 years ago, it is therefore possible that many of the rock-paintings and carvings are also very old. At all events, the Spanish chroniclers who arrived with the Conquest also describe symbolic art forms executed on rock and stone. And indeed these forms are ubiquitous on the subcontinent, with sites discovered in the Andes, the mountains of Guiana, and the river systems of the Orinoco and Amazon.

But perhaps the most impressive specimens are to be found in the equatorial forests of eastern Colombia, where they represent a living element in the culture of the indigenous tribes, even though they no longer practise the art themselves. Today the Indians there associate them with various concepts in their magic and religious beliefs. The jungle in these areas is inhabited by a variety of ethnic groups belonging to the linguistic family of the Tukano, Arawak or Carib.

Topographically, their territory is characterised by the flat-topped mountains called *mesetas*. These mountains, which are covered with dense vegetation, are remnants of the Guiana Shield and play an important part in Indian mythology. The marginal character of the region is compounded by the many rapids, waterfalls and deep gorges. In order to examine the rock-paintings and engravings one has to spend several weeks travelling in a dugout. The paintings are mostly found on rock-faces of quartzite on the upper reaches of the rivers Inírida and Guayabero, while the petroglyphs or rock-carvings have been discovered on large blocks of granite in the rapids of the rivers Vaupé and Caquetá. And they are visible for only a brief period each year, when the water level in the rivers sinks sufficiently to uncover the rocks.

Waterfalls and rapids often function as territorial borders and mythical sites. On the Río Pirá-Paraná, the Indians regard these *cachiveras* as the birthplaces of the different tribes or as the abode of the 'Lord of the Fish'. And the shamans, once they have attained a state of trance, can make contact with this spirit and ask him for permission for the Indians to fish.

The most spectacular specimen of rock-carving is to be seen above the Beijú waterfall on the middle course of the Pirá-Paraná. On the smooth vertical face of a huge block of granite, there is a symmetrical engraving known as Nyi to the local Indians. The work represents a triangular face, which the Indians interpret as a vagina, and a highly stylised figure in the form of a phallus. The site is located more or less on the Equator, and the symbols are derived from the Indian mythology of the Creation, with the phallic axis of the globe connecting the earth with the heavens and the underworld. On the other side of the rock, two sets of concentric rings have also been carved into the stone. From one of them a number of lines radiate outwards. Our guides described these two motifs as the sun and the moon, which play a dominant part in the Indians' astral mythology.

70 This beautiful carving, known as Nyi, is located on a block of granite in the Pirá-Paraná. Height 1.4 metres.

73 Top: The jungle of the Pirá-Paraná.
Bottom: Symbolic representations in high relief. The Indians associate all the petroglyphs in this region with their own mythology.

74/75 The rings symbolise the sun and the moon, which are supernatural beings in traditional Tukano mythology.

76 Rock carvings near the Caruru rapids. The Indians interpret the round depressions as the imprint of the sacred *yuruparí* instruments.

77 This engraving represents *Sebero rmu*, a mythological being who is said to have seized the *yuruparí* pipes from the women at the dawning of the world and thus initiated male supremacy.

How the moon got its spots

For the Makuna Indians, for example, the sun and moon are two mythical male figures with an ambivalent role. The Indians derive the moon's negative qualities from a mythical event, namely an act of incest committed by the moon with his sister Méneri-yo, for which she punished him by daubing paint in his face. Thus the lunar spots symbolise a transgression, so that a natural phenomenon is given a moralising role. And it is interesting that for all the ethnic groups in this region, the custom of exogamy, in which the men are compelled to marry outside their own tribal group, is strictly observed. Thus the rock images serve as a constant reminder of ethical norms rooted in myth.

We also found important sites of ancient Indian rock carvings in the area inhabited by the Cachivera Caruru. These petroglyphs are thought to be related to the theme of the sacral *Yurupari* Instruments, which again constitute a central element in the ritual of these Indians.

In one complex ceremony, a female shaman called Romi kumu appears as the original owner of the sacral flutes and trumpets that symbolise female domination over the male. In this remote mythological period, as our guides explained, the female element in fact ruled over the male. The traditional story clearly illustrates the social message in this myth: "A male spirit, Sebero, seized the instruments from the women and thus instituted male domination over the female. When Romi kumu saw Sebero, she was so afraid that she hid the *Yurupari* between her legs to hide it. The *Yurupari* is the woman's vagina." The events re-

78

A rock carving of the star spirit *nokoro rmu* on the Pirá-Paraná.
Left: A carving of the sun in south Venezuela.

lated in this mythical account raise the question whether these tribes have matriarchal tendencies.

Several times a year, the Tukano Indians hold big celebrations with these sacral *Yurupari* Instruments, which have to be kept concealed from female eyes. The 'male' trumpets are made of bark twisted into a spiral with a thick piece of cane as a mouthpiece, while the 'female' flutes are cut out of paxiuba wood smoothed down with loving care. The shrill sounds of the flutes and the muffled wailing of the trumpets are meant as a reminder of the events at the beginning of the world and as an admonition to observe the prescribed social norms.

The stone blocks and slabs in the Caruru rapids are engraved with symbols that the Indians connect with this ritual. Apart from Sebero, who seized the *Yurupari* Instruments from the women, there are two concentric rings, representing the imprint of the trumpets. The circular depression is explained as the imprint of the mouthpiece of the paxiuba pipe.

It is an open question, of course, to what extent the interpretations offered by today's Indians correspond to the intentions of the artists who created these petroglyphs so many years ago.

Interpretation is less of a problem in the case of the rock-paintings. Animal forms are the most common motifs, and they may be connected with conjurations from the Indians' hunting ritual. Some researchers, however, suggest that the shamans painted the rocks with animal symbols in order to acquire their magic fertility powers. It is thought that some motifs, which appear again and again on stones and rock-faces, were created under the influence of hallucinogens.

Many specimens of this ancient Indian rock-art have already been damaged or destroyed by weathering, while others have suffered at the hands of men. There is therefore an urgent need to protect these mysterious vestiges of the misty past of man, when the stones were not yet silent, so as to preserve them intact for future generations.

81 Rock carvings on the Pirá-Paraná.
Top: Spirits associated with the *yuruparí* rites.
Bottom: A labyrinth.

82/83 This picture, which is called Nyi, is engraved on a block of granite in the Beiju rapids. Near the site is the Equator, which forms the vertical link with the stars and the cosmic zones in Indian mythology. The Desana Indians see the stylised figure as the phallic axis of the world and the triangular face as a vagina.

80

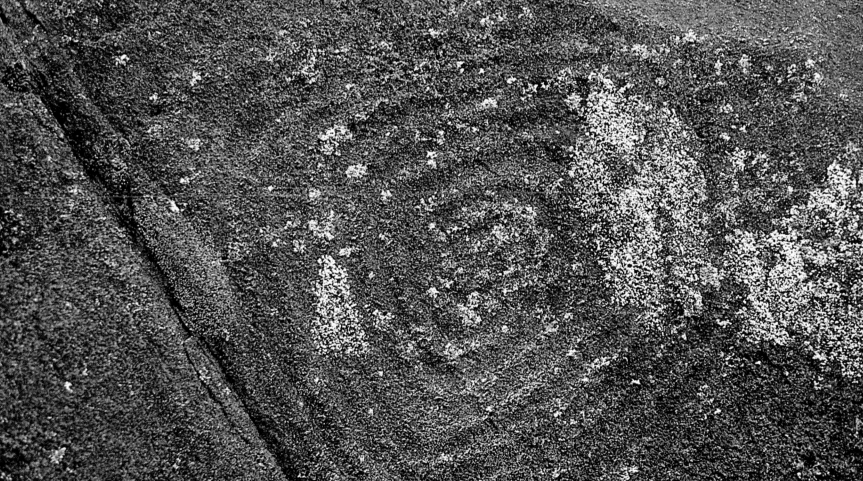

The Tukano

The Tukano Indians inhabit the little-known rain forests in the north-west of the Amazon basin. This jungle region, which is drained by the rivers Vaupés and Caquetá, is partly Colombian and partly Brazilian territory.

In the dry season the water level in the rivers drops considerably, making travel by canoe a very arduous undertaking in view of the dangers involved in overcoming the many rapids and cataracts. And when the rainy season ends in December, the *igarapé,* the tiny creeks that constitute the tributaries of the Vaupés, dry up, making it impossible to cross the watershed between the Vaupés and the Caquetá in a dugout with outboard and full equipment, and thus reach the headwaters of the Pirá-Paraná. We therefore had to hurry if we were to reach the area we wished to study in time, namely the Río Pirá-Paraná, where various tribal groups have preserved many aspects of their traditional culture and lifestyles.

The name Tukano is used to designate a whole number of ethno-linguistic subgroups, whose cultures have much in common, even though they do not form a homogeneous unit. Their main representatives are the Desana, Cubeo, Tatuyo, Barasana and Makuna. The individual groups or sibs live in communal houses called *malocas,* which are spaced out along the river at a distance of several hours by canoe from each other. For the Indians of this region, this self-imposed geographical isolation has the advantage of guaranteeing optimum use of the land and of the natural food supply.

As their economic base, the Tukano Indians grow bitter manioc, *Manihott utilissima.* They also cultivate sweet potato, peanut and plantain. Unlike sweet manioc, bitter manioc has poisonous tubers containing hydrocyanic acid. The Indians' technique for preparing the plant for human consumption is one of their great cultural achievements, without which many tribes would not have been able to survive in the jungle at all. The procedure is begun by placing the poisonous tubers on a grater encrusted with stone chippings or on a rough stone and grating them. An elaborately woven, elastic tube is then used to squeeze out the poisonous juice, and the remaining

pulp is baked in the form of round flat cakes. The Tukano women spend up to six hours a day on making this *casabe*. For protein, the men go hunting and fishing. To some extent, traditional hunting methods with the blow-gun and poisonous darts are still in use, but one also finds shotguns everywhere, which the Indians acquire from skin traders and rubber tappers. Unfortunately the traders are always encouraging them to shoot game not just for food but also for the skins, and as a result some species have already become very rare, like the jaguar, coypu and otter. In fact these animals are protected by national conservation laws, but the sheer size of the jungle makes enforcement problematical. On Brazilian territory of Amazonia alone, the authorities confiscated no less than 23,000 skins during a major sweep in 1976.

Hunting rites and ecological balance

Before the Indians go hunting, they have to observe certain rituals, because the act of killing a wild animal is otherwise considered evil. To the Tukano, all the animals of the forest and rivers are the responsibility of a powerful spirit who is lord of the animals. In the Makuna tribe, for example, the shaman or *payé* appeals to Wai masá, the Master of Animals, for permission for the Indians to hunt and kill game. If they fail to consult the spirit before setting out on a hunt, or if they kill too many animals, they must expect Wai masá to avenge the offence, which he can do by sending illness or poisonous snakes or by calling upon tornadoes to devastate their homes and crops.

Clearly, the function of this ritual is to preserve the ecological balance between

Fishermen in their dug-out.
Left: Taiwano hunter with blow-gun.

man, animals and the environment. The view of the world communicated to the hunters in their religion and magical traditions includes a biosphere with limited potential as a source of energy and fertility. If too much game is taken, therefore, the harmony of the natural cycles will be disrupted. This explains the importance of the shaman's charms and magical rites as an attempt to increase the fauna and stimulate fertility. Thus he sends the *ösi*, or souls, of the dead animals back to Wai masá in the 'House of Animals'. The Tukano believe that the animals live in a huge *maloca* with the shape of a jungle hill, which is interpreted as the womb of nature. In his trance the shaman visits the female animals there while they are asleep and cohabits with them so as to create new life.

This strong element of sexualism in their mythology is a typical feature of the Tukano religion. In his standard work on the subject, Reichel-Dolmatoff (1974: 218) discusses this sexualist content: "In all of these sexual interpretations of the animals ... we must not think for a minute of obscene comparisons in terms of our own culture. The native establishes the similarities and symbolism with deep concern; the animals of the forest and of the river are his food, they are the givers of life and of energy, and thus they form an essential part of the great procreative circuit of the biosphere and of its transcendental projections."

In addition to his role as a conserver in the energy cycle and agent of fertility, the shaman also practises a number of cult and ritual activities that accompany every member of the tribe from the cradle to the grave.

The Tukano distinguish between different kinds of shaman, or *payé* as they are called in north-west Amazonia, namely the *yai,* or jaguar, and the *kumú.* The main characteristic of a *payé* is his ability to change into a jaguar. He achieves this transformation under the influence of drugs by invoking the spirit of the jaguar from which he has received the *yai wawe,* the jaguar skin which he wears inside out. For this reason it is always dangerous for a hunter to kill a jaguar because he never knows whether it is a jaguar spirit, whose vengeance is to be feared.

Liana of the soul

A *shaman* makes use of hallucinogens in order to attain the visions which are his most important source of knowledge. "When we drink *yagé,"* say the *payé* on the Pirá-Paraná, "things begin to speak to us, and our souls are released from our bodies."

In the *lengua geral* of the Vaupés, the most efficacious drug, which is used throughout Amazonia, is called *yagé.* The Quichua word is *ayahuasca,* which means 'liana of the soul', while western scientists know it by its Latin name *Banisteriopsis caapi.*

84 In the area of the Apaporis big masked celebrations are held when certain fruits and crops are harvested. A Makuna Indian wears a bark-cloth mask with features modelled in resin. The mask represents a fish spirit.

89 The wall of a Makuna *maloca* decorated with mythological motifs. These mural docorations are now restricted to a few very isolated areas. The photograph shows Adyaba, a supernatural being who plays a central role in the Indians' creation mythology.

90/91 Tatuyo Indians making coca powder. The green leaves of the coca shrub are first roasted in a clay burner, then ground in a mortar and finally mixed with the ash of certain palm leaves in a ratio of one to one.

92 The hard work of grating the poisonous manioc tubers on a rough stone slab to produce the pulp from which the round flat cakes called *casabe* are baked. After grating, the pulp, which contains hydrocyanic acid, is squeezed out in an elastic tube to remove the poison.

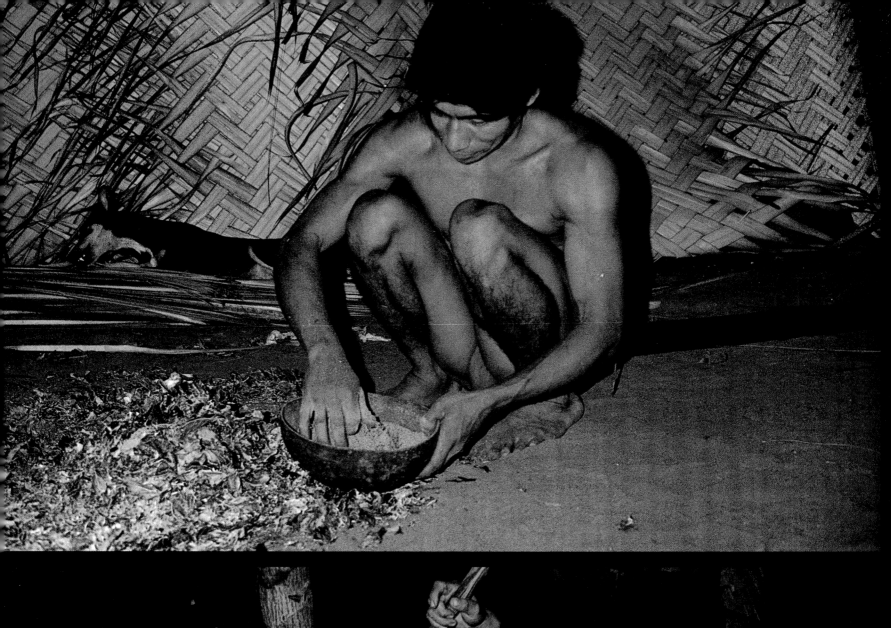

No matter what the name, the effect of the drug is the same: it leads to nausea, diarrhoea, and above all a visionary state. In his hallucinatory condition, the shaman can make contact with the tribe's ancestors and the world beyond. Our informants related how they had flown like birds and seen giant bats, huge jaguars or anacondas, and also certain psychedelic colours. Mythical figures appear to them in their trance and speak. The shamans can even enclose themselves in a bubble of air und so enter the sacred waterfalls und descend to the river bed, where they negotiate for days on end with the Master of the Fish.

Thanks to the research work conducted by ethnologists and botanists in the jungles of the Vaupés, we are now able to appreciate the importance of the fact that Indian art is based on the indigenous tribes' use of drugs. On the walls of the *malocas* and on various implements used in their magical or religious rites, such as masks, dancing staffs, bark-cloth aprons or the rattles of the shamans, one finds the same motifs again and again. Even the motifs of the Indian rock paintings are thought to be related to this prototypical 'trip'. The various painted or carved designs involving circles, dots, spirals and rhombi standing on end, as well as various stylised figures, are known to symbolise mythical beings and supernatural concepts. To the Tukano Indians, rows of dots represent human semen and the rhombus the female reproductive organs. In his detailed study of the Indians' hallucinatory experiences, Reichel-Dolmatoff provides a primarily sexual interpretation, quoting an Indian who has been brought up by missionaries: "Drinking *yagé* is a form of spiritual coitus, of spiritual union, as the priests say."

This aspect is also clearly present in the use of another drug, a narcotic snuff that is derived from a species of *Virola*. The shamans take the snuff with the help of a tubular bone, with two of them blowing the powder into each other's nostrils. Alternatively, one shaman can sniff the powder alone with the help of a fork-shaped snuff machine.

In fact there are various kinds of snuff which are kept in a separate container made from a snail-shell. They are known as *viho* and *mino,* while the Yanomami Indians on the upper Orinoco have a similar narcotic snuff that they call *ebena.*

Seed of the sun

Reichel-Dolmatoff relates the following account of the mythological origins of the narcotic snuff: "At the beginning of the world, Sun Father committed incest with his daughter, who obtained *viho* by rubbing her father's penis. In this way the

Desana received the sacred snuff from the seed of the sun, which is stored in the *muhipu neri,* the 'penis of the sun'."

Viho is the shamans' most important vehicle of communication with the world of the supernatural. It is employed for medical, magical and prophetic purposes.

In addition to *yagé* and the narcotic snuff, whose function is largely ritualised, coca *(Erythroxylon coca)* is an important stimulant. The green coca powder, which is made from the leaves of the coca shrub, is essential to the Indians in warding off hunger and fatigue. The men chew the powder for hours on end, and everyone who is invited to enter a *maloca* is welcomed with a *mambeada,* that is a helping of coca powder, which the visitor shovels into his mouth and chews slowly. For the Tukano Indians chewing coca is not just a physical act; it also symbolises the intake of magical forces. As they put it, "We cannot live without coca."

During our visit to the Pirá-Paraná we were able to witness several dances, which are of central importance as ceremonial reunions. The biggest gatherings in this region are called *dabucurí,* which may be attended by up to a hundred persons from various local phratries of the individual tribes. During the celebrations a number of functionaries can be distinguished with a variety of ceremonial roles to play, such as the precentors, dance masters, healers and, of course, the *payé.*

And this ritual specialisation is a characteristic feature of these Indians that is particularly apparent during their various celebrations.

The social structure of the tribe is also symbolised in a number of pantomimic dances. In the 'Dance of the Anaconda', for example, the dancers represent the hierarchy of the individual sibs in accordance with their creation mythology. The men line up behind each other with their hands on the shoulders of the man in front. Their rhythmic movements are an imitation of the mythical snake, with the individual dancers symbolising the individual sibs. The first dancer represents the anaconda's head, that is the highest-ranking sib.

The host of the gathering is expected to let his guests make use of his valuable feather finery, consisting of magical feathers taken from spirits in the shape of birds. And before they put on these feathers, these spirits must first be invoked. By wearing these exquisite feathered bands and splendid feather crowns, the dancers increase the magical powers of the *maloca* household and thus contribute to the success of the celebration. During the celebrations the dancers re-

Right: A Makuna making the hood of a mask. He uses his machete to apply the heated resin to the bark-cloth hood and model the actual face of the mask.

peatedly make use of hallucinogens and attempt to attain a collective state of trance by chanting mythical texts. In these incantations, the men sometimes speak in a highly ritualised language that has not yet been researched.

The magic of masks

The jungle areas of north-west Amazonia are famous not only as the home of the *dabucurí* but also as a centre of traditional South American mask rites.

The bark-cloth masks of the Cubeo Indians, for example, which they wear in connection with their funeral rites, are famous for their high artistic standards. The masks represent spirits and demons, whose task is to ward off evil powers during the funeral ceremonies. After the ceremony, the masks are stood on the open ground of the village and burnt to the accompaniment of loud wailing and moaning. This is to prevent the demons from returning when the funeral rites have been completed.

In the last few years such masks have occasionally appeared in the souvenir shops of Bogotá and Manaus in a scaled-down version, so that they can be more conveniently transported by air. Thus the commercialisation of indigenous art has now reached the jungles of the river Vaupés.

97   The painted central post, or 'ancestral post', of a Cubeo *maloca* on the Río Cuduyarí.

98/99   A pair of Cubeo masks of painted bark-cloth. The two masks represent parrot demons, whose function is to drive off the spirits of the dead during funeral celebrations.

100   The host at a *dabucurí* ceremony of the Barasana Indians produces his precious feather finery. These splendid feathered bands and crowns are a expression of the cultural wealth of the group.

101   By wearing the feathered ornaments, the dancers increase the magical powers of the sib.

102/103   The *dabucurí* begins with a dance along the 'dance path' inside the house. The men and women follow a master of ceremonies, who determines the sequence of steps and the rhythm. The dancers have gourd rattles or *maracas,* which they shake in time to the rhythm.

104   A Makuna playing on a sacred *yuruparí* flute. For all the Tukano tribes in Colombia and Brazil, the *yuruparí* rituals play a central role in their religious life.

Another kind of masked ceremony is observed by the Makuna Indians on the Río Apaporis and also among the tribes of the Mirití-Paraná. These masked dances are a part of harvest-festival rites for certain crops and are held from January to March. The Makuna wear their masks, representing the spirits of various animals and plants, in an attempt to influence supernatural beings. The rites involve a clearly sexual component illustrated in the text of the songs and the appearance of a dancer with an outsize phallus made of wood, and their function is to stimulate the fertility of the flora and fauna.

Each mask represents a supernatural creature called *rmu*. The Indians do not have a separate word for the mask itself because they do not see it as just a mask but as the embodiment of spirit.

The Makuna Indians distinguish between several different *rmu*, which can all be used at one of their ceremonies. The *nokoro rmu* is a fish spirit. *Nokoro* is the name of a small fish to which the Indians attribute sexual significance because it touches the body of human beings in the

Below: A group of males entering a *maloca* with their *yuruparí* instruments (Koch-Grünberg 1909: 315).
106/107 The Barasana prepare for a celebration.

water with its mouth. The mask comprises a hood of bark cloth with a built-up face. The *burero rmu* represents a bird spirit. It is cylindrical in shape, elaborately painted and has interchangeable ears made of light wood. The *yai rmu* is a jaguar spirit. The head is carved of light wood and covered with black resin, while earth-coloured paint is applied to imitate the pattern of the jaguar skin.

As we see, the Tukano are an Indian people whose varied use of symbolism and complex religious and philosophical concepts show how little justification there can be for the unthinking acceptance of stereotypes about the primitive mind of the Indians. Lest there be any misunderstanding about the present situation of the Tukano Indians, however, it should be stressed that contact with the white man has led to the disappearance of many aspects of their culture. The rubber tappers in particular have played no small part in accelerating the decline of their culture through shameless exploitation and a deliberate policy of creating a state of material dependence. During our extensive visits to the Tukano we have had repeated opportunities to see how the old and new, profance and sacred, now coexist. One should be mentally prepared to hear the ritual incantations of the *payé* suddenly interrupted from a corner of the *maloca* by the sweet strains of Frank Sinatra.

109 A shaman or *payé* takes several pinches of hallucinogenic snuff with the help of a snuff fork.

110/111 Barasana males collect for a ritual round of *yagé.* Under the influence of this drug they then invoke together the spirits of their forefathers and recite their genealogies. In between they refresh themselves with *cashiri,* a highly alcoholic form of *chicha* made from manioc, which they drink from large gourds.

Building with Nature

INDIAN ARCHITECTURE ON THE AMAZON

For many years, only pre-Columbian buildings of the Inca, Maya or Aztecs were regarded as aesthetic examples of Indian architecture. Unlike these monumental stone ruins, the traditional Indian forms of vernacular architecture in the Amazon basin were considered primitive, backward and dirty. Is was only much later that ethnological studies of the Tukano, Maquiritare and Cayapó Indians revealed the complexity of the factors that determine architectural styles in the equatorial rain forest. In fact, the anonymous architecture of these Indians is not just determined by practical considerations but is also closely connected with their religious beliefs and socio-economic make-up. In recent research it has been possible to demonstrate the importance of the Indians' mythology and magico-religious symbolism as well as their social structure for the construction of a building, the choice of the site, the arrangement of the settlement, the places allocated to the individual families in a communal dwelling, and also the artistic decoration of their homes.

The traditional architectural forms of the South American Indians are varied, from a simple wind-break to pile dwellings and huge communal houses that accommodate up to several hundred people. But their architecture always has one thing in common: a simple beauty that blends harmoniously with the tropical environment of the equatorial forest. All the materials required for their buildings were taken from the jungle. Certain species of tree were used for the door posts and palm leaves for the roof, while the walls were made of bamboo or chonta wood and the whole structure was held together by specially selected liana. With this exclusive use of natural materials and their architectural talent, the Indians were able to create optimum thermostatic conditions. The interior of a communal Indian house is always surprisingly cool and snuggy.

In the last few years, however, these traditional forms of Indian architecture have been almost totally abandoned in the wake of modernisation programmes and a naive belief in progress western-style. In many areas of tropical South America, the indigenous peoples have exchanged their typical Indian homes for tin huts and wooden shacks. The new form of housing taken over by the Jivaro (Shuar) on the upper Amazon may serve to illustrate the negative consequences inherent in this development. Their huts are now so small that they can accommodate only one family. Since it is considered primitive to live on the bare ground, the huts have been built on platforms. This has disadvantages with regard to hygiene and the inside temperatures. Whereas the dirt from domestic animals and small children used simply to be swept out of

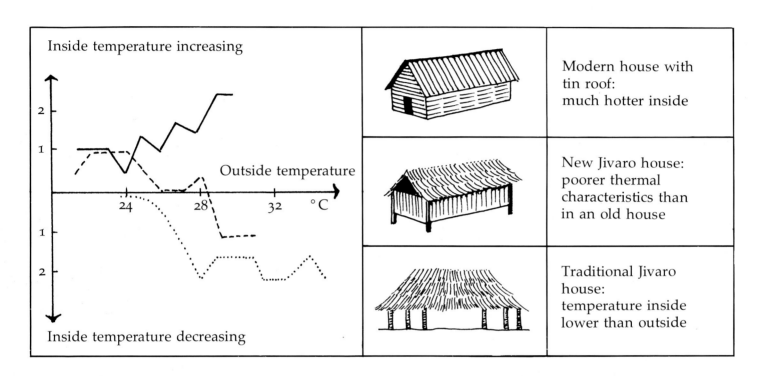

	Modern house with tin roof: much hotter inside
	New Jivaro house: poorer thermal characteristics than in an old house
	Traditional Jivaro house: temperature inside lower than outside

Inside temperature increasing

2

1

Outside temperature

24   28   32   °C

1

2

Inside temperature decreasing

the house with a broom, it now collects in the bamboo platform. In the traditional houses the hearth maintained a pleasant warmth during the night and also drove out the mosquitoes, but now the hearth is located in a kitchen that is divided off from the living room.

The following diagram illustrates the differences between the temperatures in a traditional house and the new constructions. The horizontal line indicates the outside temperature and the vertical line the temperature differences inside a traditional house, a new house and a new house with a tin roof. As the diagram shows, temperatures inside a traditional house actually decrease with a rise in outside temperature, whereas the temperature inside a new house increases relative

Temperatures in houses old and new (from Münzel 1977: 198).
Right: Impressions of an Auca house.

to the outside temperature. The house with the tin roof is of course the hottest of all.

The disappearance of traditional architectural forms therefore represents a drop in the Indians' housing standards. But it also represents a sad cultural loss, because, among other things, the new huts are no longer big enough for the traditional dances to be held there. And they used to form the social and religious basis of the Indians' communal spirit. Thus buildings of symbolic cosmic significance have often degenerated into slums on the fringe of civilisation.

The *shabono* of the Yanomami

The village form developed by the Yanomami Indians on the upper Orinoco is a unique construction of great harmony that constitutes one of the most remarkable examples of Indian architecture on the South American subcontinent. These settlements, or *shabonos,* as they call them, are made up of a continuous ring of windscreens that comprise just a monopitch roof and accommodate one family group each. The sloping roofs are arranged so as to leave an open circular or elliptical space in the centre of the *shabono,* which can be anything between twenty and eighty metres in diameter, and also to shield the Indians completely from the outside world. In addition the *shabono* ist often surrounded by a single or double palisade made of tree trunks. The living areas for the individual families have no partitions, and sometimes the individual huts merge into one unit, forming an unbroken area of roof.

For the Yanomami, the *shabono* is more than a form of protection against the elements or hostile neighbours; it is also a symbolical representation of their mythological conception of the structure of the cosmos and the universe. In their ritual songs, the *shabono* is seen as an image of the microcosm. The sacred village centre is the platform of communication between this world and the world

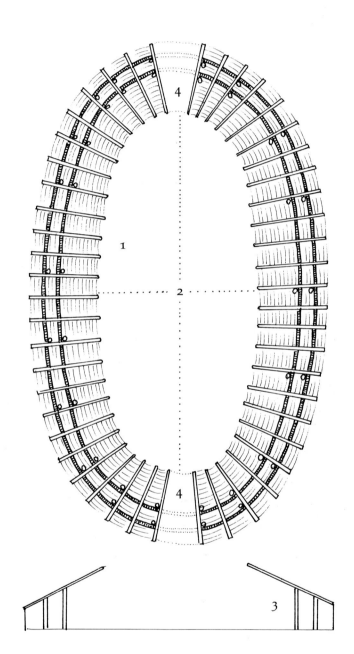

Plan of a *shabono* in the Sierra de Parima.

1 *shabono:* 'open area', 'courtyard'.
2 *muama:* The cosmic axis of the world passes through the centre of the *shabono.*
3 The 48 monopitch roofs of the family units form an unbroken covered area. They can reach a height of 6 to 8 metres.
4 Entrances.

Right: The entrance to a *shabono.*

beyond; it is the site of the cosmic *Axis mundi* that links the heavens and the underworld. From above the universe brings life and light to the interior of the *shabono,* which is open on all sides to the village, and seals it off on the outside against the darkness and dangers of the jungle.

In the arrangement of the living space it affords, the *shabono* represents a prototypical form of the social unit in pre-industrial society. Between 50 and 150 persons can live in such a village, with each family occupying a separate sector under the sloping roof, which helps mould them into a socio-economic unit.

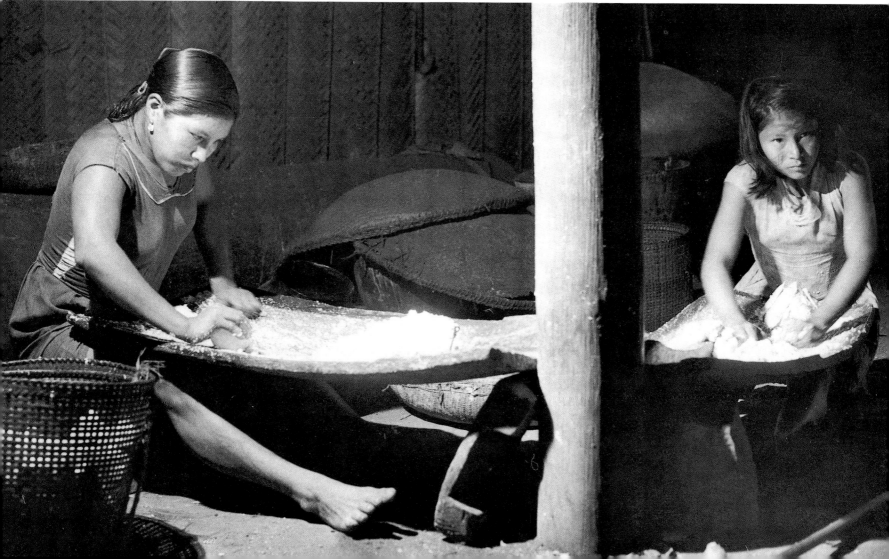

The *maloca*

The traditional dwelling of the Indian tribes in north-west Amazonia is a communal house called *maloca,* in which up to a hundred people can live. For the Tukano Indians the *maloca* is more than just a protection against the elements: it is designed to symbolise the world and the cosmos and is the centre of their lives from the cradle to the grave.

The construction of such a communal house is in fact viewed as a religious act related to the Creation Myth. In his study of the Desana Indians, Reichel-Dolmatoff explains that they interpret the *maloca* as the uterus of a sib, which is a striking example of how architecture is used to express symbolically the relationship between man and the cosmos, between the world of matter and the world of the spirit.

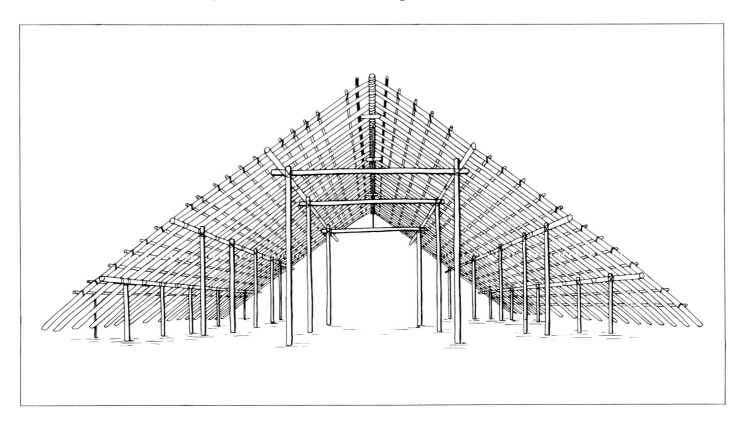

Frame of a *maloca* on the Río Vaupés (Koch-Grünberg 1909: 73).
Top left: a Makú *maloca* on the Colombian-Brazilian border.
Bottom: Daily chores inside a *maloca:* two girls busily grating the bitter manioc tubers.

In a traditional *maloca* several families live together under one roof. These families comprise an exogamic patrilineal sib that represents an independent domestic unit in a given territory.

119

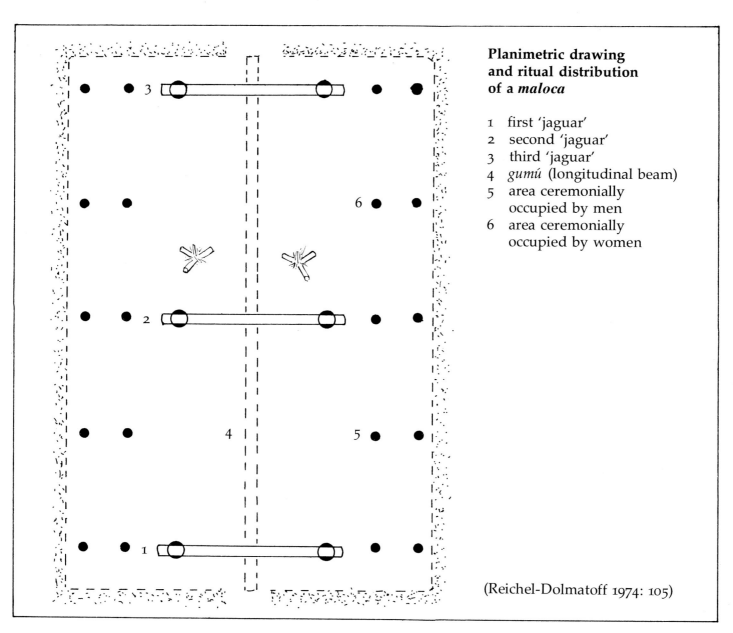

**Planimetric drawing
and ritual distribution
of a *maloca***

1 first 'jaguar'
2 second 'jaguar'
3 third 'jaguar'
4 *gumú* (longitudinal beam)
5 area ceremonially
  occupied by men
6 area ceremonially
  occupied by women

(Reichel-Dolmatoff 1974: 105)

In the area of the Río Vaupés the typical *maloca* is rectangular on plan and has a roof that slopes well down to the ground. They sometimes reach impressive proportions, up to thirty metres in length, twenty metres wide and ten metres high. The Tukano Indians build their communal houses in a jungle clearing, and a number of paths radiate out from there to the *chagras*, or plantations, and to the hunting grounds. The most important reference when constructing a *maloca* is the position of the local river and the landing place, which must always be located directly opposite the main entrance to the house.

112 A Yanomami covering the frame for the monopitch roof with palm leaves. All the work on the *shabono* is carried out by all the men on a co-operative basis.

121 A painted *maloca* of the Cubeo Indians on the Río Cuduyarí. The decorations and motifs are derived from experiences with drugs and are painted on the wall of the house by the shamans. A *maloca* houses several families under one roof, who thus form a tightly knit community.

122/123 Particularly beautiful paintings on the wall of a communal house of the Makuna on the Río Pirá-Paraná. The depicted scenes represent events in their creation mythology.

124 Old and new stilt houses of the Paraujano Indians in the Sinamaica Lagoon, Venezuela.

125

This is because the river with the landing place represents the Indians' link with the underworld, which is also their paradise. Indeed, there ist not much about the arrangement of a *maloca* that is purely fortuitous. Thus while the front door is the men's entrance, the back door is for the women. And inside the house, too, there are areas that are reserved either for the men or for the women.

In general, the interior of a *maloca* is considered a sacral place, and all the main architectural features are charged with symbolism.

The most important elements in this structure are the three pairs of forked posts connected by lateral beams that are called the 'three red jaguars'. These mythical jaguars are interpreted as the guardians of the house and the bearers of the fertility that derives from the sun. Another major structural feature is the horizontal central beam that connects the 'jaguars' longitudinally. This central beam, or *gumu*, symbolises the axis that unites the various cosmic levels. On the outside, a *maloca* is surrounded by a magically protected area that the Desana Indians interpret as a placenta. In a few very remote areas, the front wall of the building is still painted with symbolic motifs representing mythical events or magico-religions concepts.

In addition to these rectangular *malocas*, there are others that are circular on plan.

The circular *maloca* of the Makuna

Splendid specimens of circular *malocas* are still to be seen along the Río Apoporis, which flows into the Río Caquetá on the border between Brazil and Colombia. During the years 1971/72 and 1975 we visited the area several times and managed to gain the confidence of Miguel Pava, a well-known shaman, who invited us into his *maloca* and initiated us in the secret traditions and cult rituals of the Makuna Indians.

Like the universe itself, the *maloca* has a vertical structure and a horizontal structure. To the Makuna, the four central posts represent the mountains, which support the heavens. The smaller lateral posts symbolise the individual sibs, who are descended from Ideh hino, the mythical anaconda. This spiritual water snake

Circular *maloca* on the Río Apaporis (photograph 1975); internal structure and ground plan (Koch-Grünberg 1910: 285).

126

came from the underworld and entered into the world through an aquatic gate situated at some rapids. It thereupon transformed itself into a human figure, and its sons are considered the forefathers of the various sibs, which are ranked hierarchically according to the order in which they were born. In the *malocas* of the Cubeo tribe, the central posts, which they also relate to their ancestors, are painted with white anthropoid figures.

The roof of the *maloca* is the limit of the microcosm, with the ridge at the top marking the end of the universe, or *umea wawero*.

The circular floor of the *maloca* represents the earth, which is subdivided into several areas in the form of concentric rings. The centre is located at the intersection of the four main posts, which also delimit

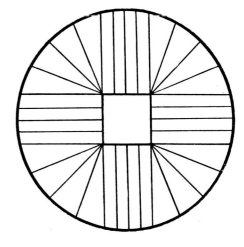

Interior of a circular *maloca* (photograph 1975); internal structure and roof (Koch-Grünberg 1910: 285).

127

the first circle. It is here, at the centre of the circle, which is the living area of the Makuna, that the shaman sits on a stool when he wishes to contact the supernatural forces. His vehicle of communication is the smoke of his huge ceremonial cigar, which rises up to the heavens along the cosmic axis.

The next zone, situated between the inner and outer circles, is called *basá ma,* the dance floor. It is here that the ceremonial dances are held.

Just as the structures and spatial relationships of the *maloca* are modelled on the mythical principles of the cosmos, so its inhabitants are seen as the descendents of those forefathers who are the main posts supporting the roof and maintain a state of harmony between man and the universe.

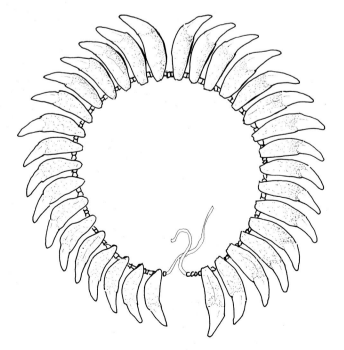

The fortified homes of the Achuar

The traditional architecture of the Jivaro on the upper Amazon is influenced not so much by religious concepts as by socio-economic constraints. While the large majority of the Shuar, the biggest of the Jivaro groups, now live in villages, the Achuar, in the border regions of Ecuador and Peru, still make use of more traditional forms.

Their original settlements, consisting of one big communal house, are still to be seen in the inaccessible area of Ipiák, Maki and Huasaga. In constructing such a settlement, the Indians had to take a number of factors into account, such as the distance from their plantations and hunting grounds, the position of the site with regard to possible flooding, and also, in case of attack, ease of defence. The houses, which are up to twenty metres long and twelve metres wide, are rectangular on plan and have rounded ends. These buildings, which are spaced at a considerable distance from each other, have no walls, being surrounded instead by three-metre-high palisades constructed out of chonta wood. Two massive gates provide the only access to these fortified homes.

Right: One of the last palisade houses of the Jivaro on the Río Bufeo, Ecuadorian Amazonia. The height of the palisade is an impressive ten feet or more.

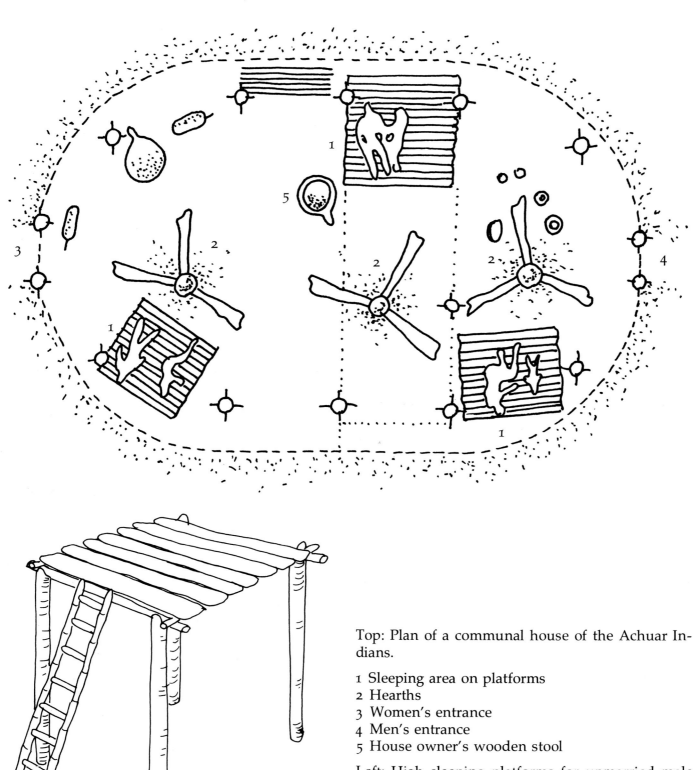

Top: Plan of a communal house of the Achuar Indians.

1 Sleeping area on platforms
2 Hearths
3 Women's entrance
4 Men's entrance
5 House owner's wooden stool

Left: High sleeping platforms for unmarried male youths (from Johnson 1977).
Top right: Achuar house without walls.
Bottom: Big clay *chicha* jugs of the Canelo Indians on the Río Curaray.

The importance of these fortifications derives from the fact that the Achuar live in a permanent state of latent war because of their constant blood feuds. No Achuar would ever leave his home without a gun. Formerly, the danger was still greater, because the head-hunting Shuar Indians regarded the Achuar as their favourite victims. In some of the fortified homes one can still find the big slit-drums that were used to transmit messages when danger threatened.

The Achuar keep the interior of their communal houses, which are usually the home of one sib, very clean and tidy. They sleep on platforms that are always placed near the hearth.

Today the Achuar Indians rarely build palisades, preferring instead to safeguard their homes by building two-metre-high walls of wooden laths. In those areas where hostilities have completely ceased, their homes have no walls at all, or alternatively they are built in the Creole style.

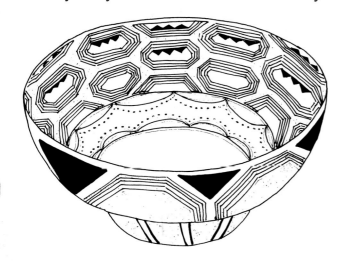

133 Top: Communal house of the Achuar on the upper Amazon.
Bottom: The interior of the house. The owner is sitting on a *chumpi*, a wooden stool, threading large birds' bones onto a belt. This shoulder strap, or *tayu*, was formerly the symbol of a successful head-hunter. To the right are the platforms of the sleeping area.

134/135 The roof construction of an Achuar house. In traditional Indian architecture, all building materials are derived from the natural environment of the tropical rain forest.

136 Two Tukano *malocas* with a rectangular plan. In a few areas of the Río Vaupés the traditional solitary settlements have been preserved.

137 Top: On the Río Aguarico in Ecuador, the Siona and Secoya Indians build their communal houses on stilts. The agglomeration of houses to form small settlements is a recent development.
Bottom: The fireplace in an Achuar house. The fire is kept burning or the ash glowing to counteract the perpetual damp and take the chill off the cold nights.

138/139 An Achuar farmstead on the Río Pastaza in Ecuador is surrounded by a huge palisade of chonta wood. In times of war the more exposed settlements are protected by several such palisades. And during the night the Jivaro let their dogs roam free between the fences as an extra protection.

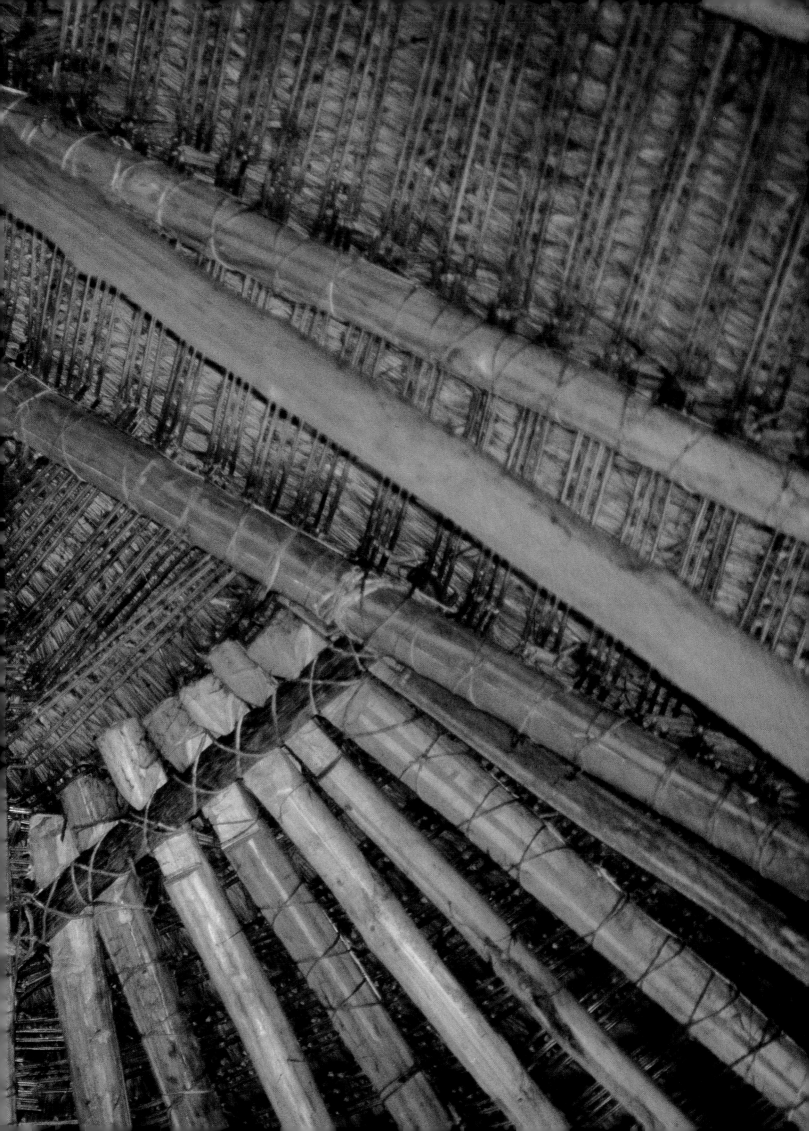

The Jivaro

Where the jungle-covered eastern slopes of the Andes merge into the vast Amazon lowlands, the Jivaro Indians have their home, in an area that straddles the border between Ecuador and Peru.

Formerly the word 'Jivaro', which is not in fact taken from the language of this tribe, was used as the name for the famous head-shrinkers from the upper Amazon. Over the centures, however, the term has developed into a synonym for 'wild Indians in the jungle'.

This remarkable people does not form a single political unit at all but rather comprises a number of sub-groups, each with a name of its own. In the jungles of the *montaña,* as their habitat is called, there live approximately 30,000 Shuar, 5000 Achuar, 18,000 Aguaruna, 5000 Huambisa and 2000 Candoshi. Many of their tribal areas lie astride the border between Ecuador and Peru.

From a cultural point of view, the Jivaro occupy a mid-position between the Indian cultures of the Amazon and the old civilisations of the Andes region. For a long time they had a reputation for being the most dangerous Indians in South America, a reputation they owed not least to their habit of cutting off their enemies' heads and then shrinking them. But the white men have never had any reason to fear them; the Jivaro reserve this custom for their Indian enemies, especially the Achuar.

For the Jivaro Indians, an enemy's head is a trophy, and taking such a tropy, or *tsantsa,* as they call it, represented a deeply religious act that fortified the powers of the soul and also conferred personal prestige. Although head hunting was seen as a blood-thirsty affair by the whites, it is worth pointing out that the Jivaro never killed for material gain. And the same cannot be said of the Europeans, such as the Puritans of New England, who paid 60 dollars for every Indian scalp, so greedy were they for the Indian territories.

In the old Jivaro culture, taking a *tsantsa* was closely bound up with a complicated mythology of the soul. In fact, as Michael Harner, an American anthropologist who lived with these Indians for many years, has pointed out, the Jivaro believe in several types of soul or life principle, which they call *wakani.*

Of course, it is often impossible to translate Indian terms and religious concepts into other languages, and here again the word 'soul' cannot be more than an approximation. In addition to the material world, many Indian tribes believe in an immaterial substance or structural principle, which can be present in human beings, animals, plants and in nature generally. They distinguish, for example, between *arutam wakani,* the acquired soul, *muisak wakani,* the avenger soul, and *nekás wakani,* the true soul, which turns into a cloud or mist after death.

The greatest importance is attached to *arutam,* however, a soul that one is not born with but which must be acquired. It is only by possessing its magical force that the Jivaro Indian can protect himself from sorcery or death in the course of an enemy attack. When only six years old, the boys accompany their fathers to the sacred waterfalls, whose magical forces reside in the spray. Together, they camp on the river bank by the waterfall for several days, and the boy bathes many times in the water from the falls. Under this paternal supervision, the boy fasts, drinks tobacco juice and takes hallucinogenic drugs so as to attain his first *arutam* visions.

Harner's description of the various stages in the acquisition of *arutam* is so vivid as to deserve quoting in the original (1973: 138–139): "If the *arutam* seeker is fortunate, he will awaken at about midnight to find the stars gone from the sky, the earth trembling, and a great wind felling the trees of the forest amid thunder and lightning. To keep from beeing blown down, he grasps a tree trunk and awaits the *arutam.* Shortly the *arutam* appears from the depths of the forest, often in the form of ... giant jaguars fighting one another as they roll over and over to the vision seeker. When the apparition arrives, the Jivaro must run forward and touch it, either with a small stick or his hand.

Upon thus achieving success in encountering an *arutam,* the person returns to his house. After nightfall, the soul of the same *arutam* he touched comes to him as he dreams. His dream visitor is in the form of an old Jivaro who says to him, 'I am your ancestor. Just as I have lived long, so will you. Just as I have killed many times, so will you.'

When one has thus obtained an *arutam* soul, he generally is seized with a tremendous desire to kill, and it is ordinarily only a matter of a few months before he joins a killing expedition."

The Jivaro men can even possess two *arutam* simultaneously, which greatly increases their strength and powers of resistance. On the other hand, this magical principle can also depart from its owner's body and in that case it must then be regained. The most important goal in the life of a Jivaro Indian, however, is to attain the status of a *kakaram,* which literally means a 'mighty one'. But he can only do so by killing the tribe's enemies, which again increases his magical powers and helps to protect him and his family.

Before a Jivaro can die while on a head-hunting expedition, his *arutam* soul must have departed from his body or else have been stolen. But when he does finally die, all the *arutam* souls he has possessed in the course of his life are released and become free to enter into other Jivaro. At the same time the soul *muisak wakani* arises, whose task it is to avenge the Indian's death.

It is to prevent this avenger soul from escaping and perhaps becoming a dangerous demon that the victim's head must be shrunk as soon as possible.

As far as we know, the procedure for preparing a *tsantsa,* a shrunken head, has only been observed by one European, namely by the *sertanista* Up de Graff in 1899.

The victim's head is first severed at the atlas. Then the bearer of the trophy, who is called *tsamkram,* passes a headband through the mouth and gaping neck for ease of transport. While still on their way home, they split the skin at the back of the head and carefully remove it, throwing the skull in the river. Then the muscle fibres are scraped away, before the skin is sewn up again using a twisted thread made of vegetable fibre. The lips are closed temporarily with three thorns and later they are sewn together. The neck is lined with an elastic strip of liana, and the head is ready to be filled again and again with hot sand, until it has shrunk to the size of a fist. During the process the face is moulded to create the desired features. The whole procedure can last several days or even weeks and the owner of the *tsantsa* must observe certain tabus throughout this period.

Today the Jivaro no longer go head-hunting, at least not recently as far as we know. But hostilities between the individual groups still continue in the form of blood feuds. The reason for this is that the Jivaro believe that illness and accidents are the work of hostile sorcerers, who must be punished.

Head-hunting and the trophy cult were also practised in the pre-Columbian civilisations of the Andes, as illustrations on ceramic vessels of the pre-Inca Nazca culture show.

During my many journeys through the territory of the Jivaro Indians I have never seen any signs of *tsantsa* being prepared nowadays. Even the Shuar Federation had to apply to an ethnological museum in Germany when they wanted to acquire a shrunken head for exhibition purposes.

From *tsantsa* to souvenir

In the first half of the twentieth century, the demand among collectors for *tsantsa* was so great that corpses were disinterred specially for the purpose of preparing *tsantsa* from the heads. At times, attempts have been made to encourage Indians to go head-hunting so as to produce more of these prized trophies. Even today the occasional head trophy appears in Quito, which raises the question where they come from. A good specimen costs about 2000 dollars today, although trade with such objects is strictly forbidden. Imitation shrunken heads made of goat skin are now a popular souvenir that can be bought all over Ecuador.

Tribal traditions of the Achuar

In the area to the east of the Cordillera de Cucutú, where the rivers from the Andes start to become more docile, live the Achuar, another group of Jivaro Indians, whose lives still follow traditional patterns. Here, on the border between Ecuador and Peru, the Achuar have only seen more of the white man and his ways in the last few years. These Indians rely for their food primarily on horticulture based on the slash and burn principle, with sweet manioc, maize, sweet potato, plantain and peanut as their basic crops.

140 A Jivaro youth with *tawasap*, a magnificent head-dress made from tufts of small feathers from several dozen toucan.

145 Achuar girl from Ipiak with her face painted.

146/147 The Achuar are renowned for their hunting skills. Their blow-guns are a prized article of trade among the neighbouring tribes.

148 Top: Loading a blow-gun. To stabilize the dart in flight, the end has cotton fibres from the kapok-tree tied to it.
Bottom: A rod is used to apply curare, a quick-working poison, to the darts, which the Indians make from the ribs of palm leaves.

149 Top: Basket weaving is a common Indian occupation.
Bottom: The cord for making nets and bags is twisted from the fibres of the chambira palm.

150 *Chicha*, the daily food of the Jivaro, is made from fermented manioc pulp and water. The women chew the manioc pulp, adding their saliva as a catalyst for fermentation.

151 A young wild pig or peccary is fed manioc pulp.

152 Top: The women are highly skilled in shaping pottery bowls for drinking *chicha*.
Bottom: The fermented manioc mash is stored in big *chicha* jugs.

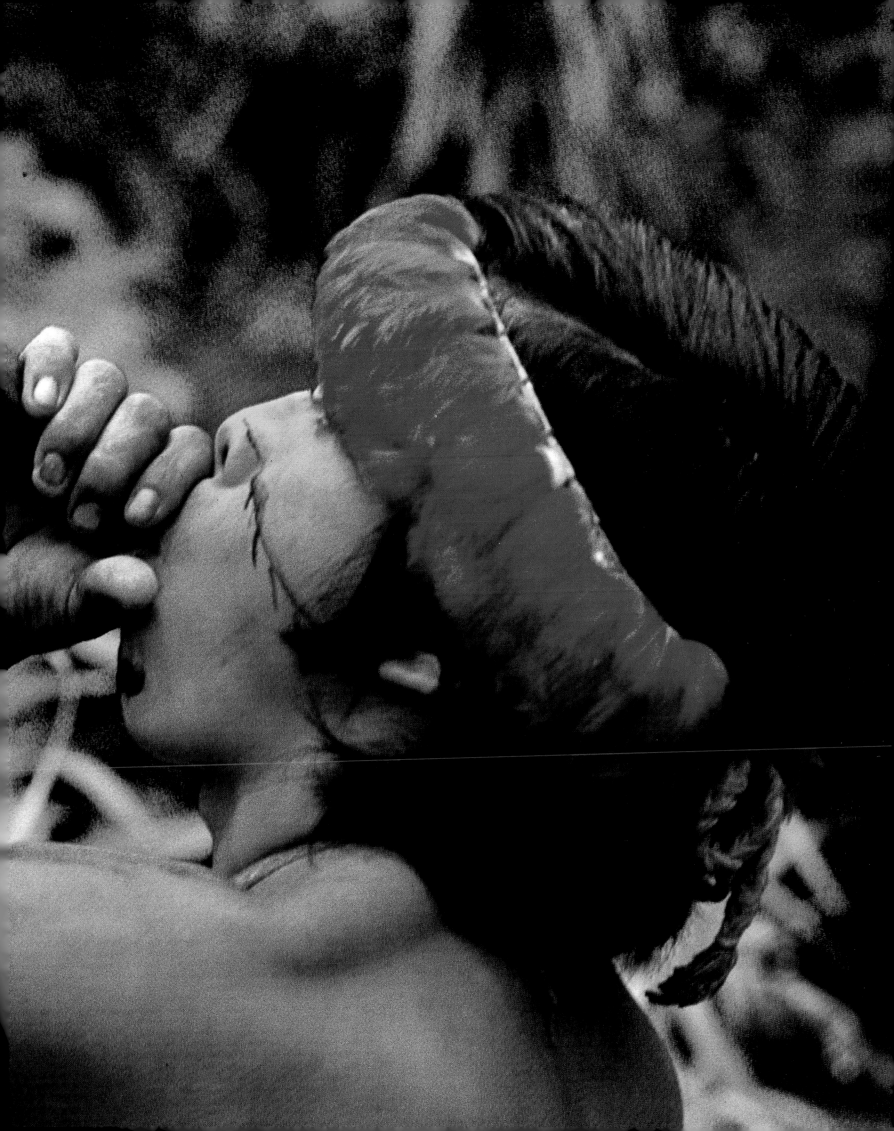

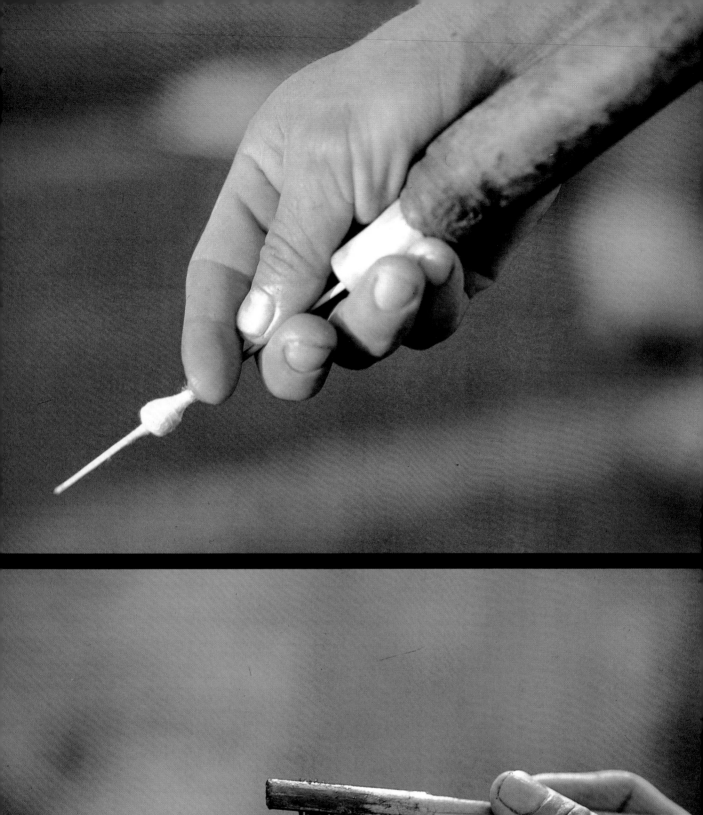

The Achuar have a reputation for being excellent hunters, and their neighbours are always keen to trade for their blow-pipes and arrow poison. The Achuar themselves now hunt with shotguns as well as blow-guns, while their dogs, which are trained specially for the purpose, also play an important part. When a dog's training is complete, his owner holds a celebration, during which the shaman blows tobacco smoke into the animal's eyes and nostrils and pours a magic potion into its mouth. This is to give the dog an excellent nose and keen sight for tracking the game. This example shows once again the close relationship that exists between the Indians and their animals, both of whom combine with the the plant world to form the metaphysical unity of the Indians' all-embracing philosophy of life.

The magic of the arrow

The key role in mediating between the tribe and the world of the supernatural is played by the medicine men or shamans. Wh the help of tobacco and hallucinogens they are able to contact the sphere of the spirits and magical powers. Their strongest drug is ayahuasca, which the Jivaro call *natema.*

In the lives of the Achuar, too, the shaman has a key role to play. In his trance he can heal the sick, predict the outcome of the hunt, and also cast evil spells. His most powerful weapons against potential enemies arc his magic arrows, or *tsetsaks,* which he shoots at his victims.

Apart from drugs, which are used primarily by the shamans, all the Achuar men imbibe a ritual purification potion xtracted from the leaves of the guayusa shrub. At one or two o'clock in the morning the men arise from the platforms that serve as their beds and assemble round the hearth. There they drink this bitter guayusa tea until they are forced to go outside and vomit, a process which the Achuar interpret as a form of physical and psychic purification. The men then remain gathered round the flickering light of the fire until the dawn, discussing the work of the coming day, potential dangers, and the possibility of an avenging raid, or rclating the themes of their magical traditions and mythology.

During our last visit to these Indians, however, their discussions were dominated by quite different topics. The big question was what would happen when the settlers came from the highlands, when there was no more hunting and fishing for the tribes of hunters and fishermen.

And the majority of them in fact decided to apply to join the Federación Shuar, an umbrella organisation for the Jivaro tribes.

Headhunters today–an example of Indian emancipation

One of the most striking characteristics of these people is the courage and determination they have shown in defending themselves against intruders, invaders and alien cultures. Before the Conquest, for example, the Jivaro put up such strong resistance to Huayna Capac, the Inca emperor, that he was forced to abandon his war of conquest and withdraw back to the Andes. The Spaniards did not fare much better; and only Macas, now the regional capital of the province of Morona-Santiago, came under colonial rule for several centuries. It is only in the last decades that the Jivaro have been confronted with the full force of western civilisation. The government of Ecuador actually declared the habitat of the Indians 'free territories', just waiting to be exploited; and the agricultural authorities worked out colonisation projects and sent groups of settlers into the jungle as a new source of *lebensraum* for the overcrowded population in the Andean highlands. Needless to say, the ensuing spontaneous acts of settlement have sometimes created conflict between the intruders and the autochthonal population.

But now, only 15 to 20 years after these colonisation projects were started, there is a reverse migration pattern back to the Andean highlands. This can be explained by the difficulties the settlers have encountered in adjusting to a less equable climate and harsher environment and, above all, to their inability to put aside their old methods of cultivation, which quickly exhaust the jungle soil. This constitutes only a thin layer of humus in the Amazon basin, so that intensive farming techniques tend to cause soil erosion. The danger of creating a steppe landscape as a consequence of the intensive sunshine and violent tropical rainstorms is also very great. These are facts of jungle life that the Indians have always taken into account, cultivating their crops by the slash and burn method. This involves clearing a stretch of jungle and burning the felled trees, leaving the ash to fertilise the soil. Then the crops are planted between the remaining tree-trunks and shrubs, which prevent the humus layer from being washed out. In addition, these fields are only cultivated for two or three years, before being left fallow for the soil to recover. Regrettably the development programmes launched for these territories, often involving the ruthless exploitation of the natural resources, like timber, rubber and oil, have failed to take account of the ecological requirements of the their Indian inhabitants.

New infrastructures, including roads, landing strips and energy supply, have primarily benefitted those who have come to exploit, while the indigenous population has gone empty-handed. The policy of integration pursued by the development agencies has not been realised, leaving the local Indians stranded on the margins of a civilisation for which they have not been prepared.

In view of this situation the Shuar Indians in Ecuador decided to help themselves and founded an umbrella organisation that could represent their interests with the greater vigour of a common purpose and so keep the spectre of proletarianisation from their door. Under the guidance of Salesian missionaries, they set up the Federación de Centros Shuar in Sucua in 1965. Today, the Federación has a membership of about 20,000 Indians, organised in 154 local groups covering approximately one third of the Amazonian area of Ecuador.

Economically, the Federación has flourished with the introduction of new agricultural policies in the jungle, such as the more intensive practice of cattle-breeding, which had only been a sporadic feature hitherto. The Federación has also had most of the traditional tribal lands surveyed and registered as collective property, which is without doubt their greatest achievement to date, as the government had previously refused to recognise the Indians' right to their land.

An interesting activity developed by this Indian organisation is a system of radio schools that it operates, differing greatly from the usual state and mission schools. In Sucua, the federation's headquarters, a variety of teaching programmes are produced, taking full account of the social context of the Indians, and they are then broadcast as complete programmes. They also publish the Fasciculos Shuar, in which cultural and social aspects of Indian life are recorded and discussed.

This separate Shuar system of education, which has since been recognised by the government, comprises an elementary and a secondary level in their own language with parallel tuition in Spanish. In these bilingual schools the teachers, all Shuar who have been specially trained for their work, receive the lessons by radio und pass them on to their pupils. The producers are at pains to base their teaching on the old social and cultural values of the Indians, including oral tradition, Indian music, and themes relating to their jungle home. Today this unique project comprises 100 radio schools with over 100 'radio teachers' giving bilingual lessons to 2,000 pupils. And the particular advantage of the system is that it can be used to reach Indian groups in the most remote areas of the jungle.

The dynamism of the Shuar and their activities today has led to changes in many aspects of their traditional culture, although these changes are not equally obvious in every area. Thus the economic adjustments they have made in their switch to a mixed system of agriculture with a stock-farming base have not been without some dangerous side-effects. A number of agricultural goods they once produced themselves now have to be purchased. And whereas the individual sibs live in isolated communal houses under the traditional system, there is now a tendency to build settlements or *caserios* comprising several family houses. The introduction of farming co-operatives and the consequent concentration of power in the hands of the tribal council has also had a profound influence on the social structure of these Indians. New forms of authority have developed, and the influence of the missionaries has increased at the expense of the standing of the medicine-men. In some cases, economic change has even led to signs of a social and economic class system.

In spite of all these problems and difficulties, however, the Shuar Indians have been very successful in their attempts to bridge the gap between the traditional life and values of the tribe and the claims of the twentieth century.

By playing an active role in the government's integration policies, on the one hand, and by developing the tools with which to preserve their cultural identity and independence on the other, the Federación Shuar has become a model example of Indian self-help throughout the whole of South America.

157   An Achuar youth.

158/159   By the light of the fire, the men assemble for the *guayusa* ceremony. An Achuar drinks the bitter extract of the leaves of the guayusa shrub from a narrow gourd. During their vigil the men indulge in ritual vomiting, personal hygiene and long discussions.

160/161   The Maki Lagoon marks the jungle border between Ecuador and Peru.

162   An Achuar from the Río Pastaza with a traditional crown of feathers, plus modern shotgun and transistor radio. The picture is symbolic of the present situation of many jungle Indians.

163   In the depths of the jungle is the radio school of Maki. From Sucua the Federación Shuar broadcasts the lessons in Spanish and Shuar to the teachers, who pass them on to their pupils.

156

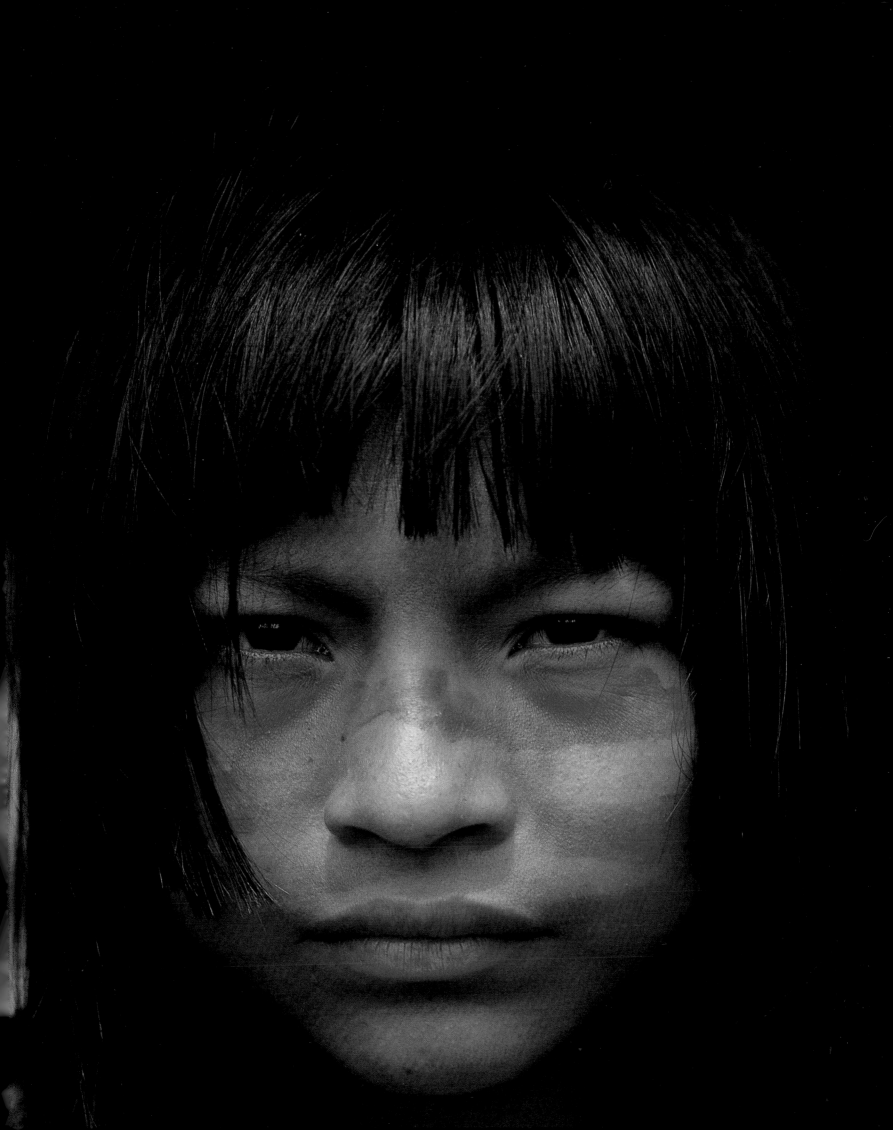

The Quichua

The Andean areas of Ecuador, Peru and Bolivia were once a centre of the most advanced cultures in South America. The year 1532, however, in which Francisco Pizarro and his men imurdered Atahuallpa, the last Inca ruler, marked the end of a splendid cultural development.

Today, the ruins of the magnificent Inca architecture, the colourful traditional dress of the Indians and the languages spoken by the indigenous peoples bear witness to the former splendour and ethnic diversity of the Andean region. The Quechua language of Peru—or Quichua, as it is known in Ecuador,—was once the official idiom of the Inca empire and is still spoken by several million Indians today. In Peru, Quechua is officially recognised as a second national language. Apart from Quechua, Aymara is still spoken in the area around Lake Titicaca and also in much of Bolivia.

The Spanish colonists did not create any new social forms but subjected the existing order to their rule and installed a system of dependence. As a result, it was the social and economic structures of the pre-Columbian Indian societies that suffered most from the Conquest. Nevertheless *minga,* the semi-collective system of mutual help, did survive in some areas.

Today the majority of the Indians in the Andes profess Christianity, but many of the ancient concepts still linger on or have combined to produce syncretic compromises with the demands of the new religion. Contact with the Spaniards was not without its effects, stimulating effects too, on the great tradition of handicrafts in the region, and many Indian artists and craftsmen have nurtured their heritage and developed new forms.

In the last few years, many South American governments have also started to take note of the artistic activities of their Indian population and have founded cooperatives and handicraft schools to promote the work of the weavers, carvers, potters and silversmiths. In order to do justice to the artistic expression of the Andean Indians, it is necessary to distinguish between handicraft and ethnographic art. The latter is only practised to satisfy the artist's and his family's personal needs and is primarily concerned with ritual objects.

Spirits wearing baseball caps

This cultural interface has often produced one very intriguing effect, as in the case of the Canelo, the lowland Quichua: a creative synthesis of traditional and alien cultural elements. An excellent example is to be found in the fine ceramics that are the typical art-form of the Canelo Indians in the Amazon basin of Ecuador.

Apart from motifs taken from their own socio-cultural situation, their art also depicts the white intruders and symbols of their power, such as bulldozers, the baseball caps worn by the oilmen working in the jungle, or missionaries in pith-helmets sitting in a dugout. Often the two elements, traditional and modern, are combined in one object, such as a figurine of a spirit wearing in all-American cap–an ironic comment, but at the same time an expansion of the traditional spiritual world in the face of a changing environment.

More recently there has also been a tendency to commercialise traditional Indian art for the souvenir trade, concentrating on motifs borrowed from Indian socio-cultural and religious life, like shrunken heads in ceramics, Auca heads with pierced ears or demons in animal form. In some cases the intention may be caricature or satire on the part of the artist. At all events they are all a product of exposure to western civilisation.

A ceramic figurine of a spirit incongruously wearing a baseball cap. The Sacha Runa Indians, or 'Forest People', as these lowland Quichua speakers call themselves, have learnt to combine the symbols of technological progress with their traditional motifs and values. Their ceramic work, including drinking vessels, *chicha* jugs, ritual figurines and cooking utensils, is done exclusively by women.

Heirs of the Inca in the northern Andes

Unlike the small, fragmentary tribal groups living in the Amazon jungle, the Quichua speaking Indians of the Andes are members of large homogeneous tribes, who share in the same linguistic tradition through their common language.

The present habitat of these Indians is an area on the edge of the vast Sierra, which is surrounded by snow-capped volcanoes and the two cordilleras, amidst a landscape of unique beauty. In the early years of the colonial period, however, they were forced to withdraw into areas with the most adverse ecological and economic conditions. The unequal division of land into latifundios and minifundios soon brought the indigenous tribes to the verge of ruin. And their situation was aggravated by laws of inheritance according to which the land had to be divided up between all the children. But even under such difficult conditions they succeeded in developing strategies for survival. Using only the simplest agricultural techniques, they cultivated the steep slopes and poor soil of the cordilleras up to 4,000 metres and more, planting maize, barley, potatoes, various tuberous roots, onions and vegetables.

Their traditional building methods also make use of the materials provided by their natural environment. The roofs of straw and walls of dried clay brick provide shelter against storm and cold, and also blend harmoniously with the countryside.

But often their little plot of land was not sufficient to feed a whole family, so that, starting with the colonial period, the Indians were often forced to work as peons, as landless field workers, on the big estates or haciendas. The Ecuadorian writer Jorge Icaza wrote a novel entitled 'Huasipungo', which is a dramatic account of the fate of the oppressed farm labourers, the *huasipungueros*. Under this system, each peon was given a small plot of inferior land to satisfy his needs, and in return he undertook to work for his master for nothing five days a week. By deliberately getting the *huasipunguero* into debt, it was possible to keep him in a state of bondage which he would never have the money to escape from all his life. It was not until 1964 that the system of *huasipungo* was abolished by law in Ecuador.

In the Sierra, the highlands of Ecuador, it is often difficult to distinguish between Indians and non-Indians. Afer 400 years of racial mix, the mestizos or *cholos*, to use the derogatory term, are genetically closer to the indigenous peoples than to the whites. Therefore the barriers separating the world of the Indians on the one hand from the world of the mestizos and whites on the other are not based on racial features but on the socio-cultural situation of the respective ethnic groups. This dualistic structure of South American society is reflected most vividly in a sociological study of the highland Indians of Ecuador. According to the authors of the study, many inhabitants of the province of Chimborazo believe that the word 'patria' (fatherland) is the name of a coach operator whose coaches drive through their territory. And in another test it was found that many of the Indians believed that the name of their country was 'Amazon'. Such research work, no matter how objective it may be, does of course run the risk of intensifying prejudice against the Indian population. But on the other hand, these examples reflect the problems that are an obstacle to good relationships between the different ethnic groups in the Andean region.

Research into the Andean Indians is hampered by the present fashion of claiming Inca forebears, a claim that is often impossible to check. But in fact, Inca rule lasted only about fifty years in Ecuador. The Salasaca Indians in the central highlands, for example, are thought to have been *mitimaes* from Bolivia. *Mitimaes* is the name given to tribes that rebelled against Inca rule and were forcibly resettled as part of their punishment. Many cultural elements have been taken over by the mestizos and form an integral part of South American folk customs.

164 The Tungurahua volcano is 16,446 feet high and is situated in the eastern cordillera of Ecuador.

169 An Otavaleña plaits her husband's hair.

170 In the Andean area celebrations often take the form of masked processions. This leather mask of a jaguar is the work of Indians in the province of Chimborazo.

171 While the traditional masks in Indian celebrations represent certain animals, other types can also be observed in the mestizo processions. The mask in the photograph represents a buffoon and is meant as an ironic comment.

172 Top: A woman from Otavalo at the spinning wheel. Weaving is an ancient art the Andean Indians already practised in the pre-Columbian era.
Bottom: Even small boys can be found working the looms, which were introduced by the Spaniards. Many of the motifs used for the wall-hangings, ponchos and scarves are not a product of Indian culture, however, but are designed to appeal to the tourists.

173 Top: Many of the Indians in the villages around Otavalo earn their living as homeworkers at the loom.
Bottom: The back-strap loom, which was common before the Conquest, is now restricted to a few areas.

174 Top: A barn in the Andean highlands.
Bottom: The poor soil is tilled with simple implements.

175 In a Quichua farmstead in Chimborazo Province, Ecuador.

176 All Saints' Day at the Indian cemetery in Otavalo. They call upon both Christian saints and their traditional Indian deities.

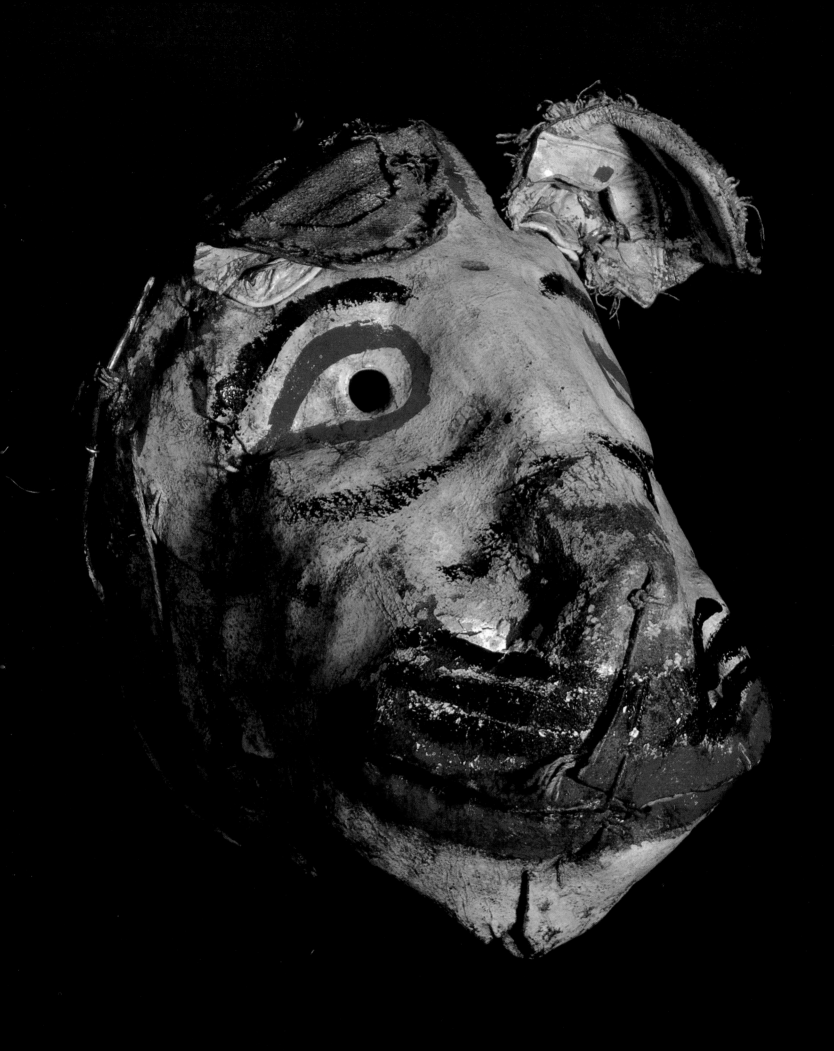

The masked processions, for example, which may be of Indian or Spanish origin, provide both ethnic groups with a wonderful opportunity to let off steam, and to reflect their social, economic and political condition at the same time. Today the masks are made of wood, cloth, papier maché, leather, wire netting and tin, and represent their Iberian conquerors, priests, the local authorities or the gringos, the foreigners.

One of the most outstanding Indian peoples in the Andean region are the Otavaleños, who live in the northern Sierra in the province of Imbabura. Thanks to their artistic talents, diligence and good business sense, they have often managed to acquire the status of traders and small-time entrepreneurs.

The Otavaleños are easily recognised by their picturesque dress, the men wearing white knee-length trousers, a thick blue poncho made of wool, sandals made of aloe fibre or rubber from old tyres, and a sombrero. The symbol of their independence and their proud male spirit is their splendid plait of hair.

For the women, traditional dress comprises the *anaco,* a dark blue or black flannel skirt, a light-coloured embroidered blouse, the *mamachumbi,* a hand-woven belt decorated with symbolic patterns, and the *fachalino,* a rectangular cloth that they drape over their shoulders or wear on their heads.

In remote villages the women still wear their beautiful old silver jewellery. This mainly comprises ear pendants, which are executed in fine filigree work and are reminiscent of the colonial period, and brooches, calles *tupos* in Quichua, which the women use to fasten their ponchos or hold their shawls in place. The traditional *tupos* of the Otavaleños take the form of a large round disc with a kind of safety pin at the back and are made of silver. The outside surface is engraved with decorative designs.

Every group of Indians in the Andes has its own kind of brooch, which can made of brass, copper, nickel or silver. Many *tupos* represent certain figures and function as a charm to protect the person wearing them. The brooches used by the Saraguro in the southern Sierra of Ecuador are especially beautiful. They are characterised by a sun motif at the head of the pin with a pattern of small heads radiating outwards. Many of these brooches are believed to continue pre-Columbian traditions, a theory that is supported by archaeological finds.

The Otavaleños are also famed throughout South America for their skill as weavers. The men go on long journeys to other countries, selling their wares. One can see them in Bogotá, Rio de Janeiro and even in New York, heavily laden with their ponchos, wall-hangings, bales of cloth, and shawls.

But it would be creating the wrong impression to suggest that all Otavaleños are successful and wealthy traders. Most of them in fact sit at home at the loom and have no entrepreneurial function.

On the other hand, there are small factories owned by Indians who employ up to sixty Indian weavers. Most of their products are exported to North America. Today orlon has largely replaced wool as the basic material, while the hand loom has usually given way to big mechanical looms.

The small-time salesmen can be seen selling their wares wherever there are tourists, although the biggest selection of textiles in the region is to be found at the Saturday market in Otavalo. However, that many of the patterns that are on sale here are not part of the cultural traditions of the Otavaleños but rather are designed specially to cater to tourist tastes.

These new forms of employment do provide an attractive source of income; but they also involve certain problems. Being so busy working at their looms, for example, the Otavaleños have no time for their crops any more and now have to purchase products they previously harvested themselves.

Sorcerers and Healers

MAGIC AND MEDICINE

When Abraham Calazacon opens the door to his hut in the jungle at two o'clock in the morning, he can be sure to find a dozen or more patients waiting to consult him. Abraham is the *Cazique,* the headman of the Colorado Indians, whose tribal name they owe to the red paste made from anatta with which they dress their hair. Everyday bus-loads of air-conditioned tourists arrive after a three-hour drive from Quito to see the picturesque Indians. Few of them, who pay four dollars a time for a shot of a bare indigenous breast, are aware of the fact that the Colorado provide Ecuador with some of their most famous medicine-men. Abraham, for example, owns his own automobile, and the fire brigade in Santo Domingo de los Colorados has made him an honorary member as a token of their gratitude for his generous donations.

Although the tribal culture of the Colorado has become highly commercialised, their healing skills are famous among the Indian tribes. From time to time secret gatherings are held in Abraham Calazacon's house, attended by the sorcerers and healers from the coastal regions, the Andean highlands and even from the lowlands of the Amazon basin. These meetings provide them with an opportunity to discuss their latest findings and to exchange medicinal herbs and hallucinogenic drugs that are only available in certain ecological zones.

Like the fetish priests of voodooism in the Caribbean region, or the witch doctors of the Afro-American cults in Brazil, the traditional healers of the Andean countries are also enjoying a renaissance at the present moment. All the Indian markets in Ecuador, Peru and Bolivia, for instance, have special stalls where they sell roots, herbs, mushrooms, stones and, in places, dried llama foetuses. The naturopaths – and they are not all Indians – use all these items in their ritual cures.

It is only very recently that scientific research into the phenomena of traditional Indian medicine has been carried out. For a long, long time the methods employed by the medicine-men and shamans were dismissed as so much hocus-pocus. But the recent studies made by doctors, ethnologists and psychologists have made people more aware of the true significance of the healers' arts.

In every traditional Indian group in South America there is someone whose function it is to mediate between man and his gods. According to which of the various ritual roles they fulfil and the different religious concepts involved, they are called shamans, medicine-men, witch doctors, sorcerers or healers.

If a woman has failed to produce a baby, if someone has bouts of dizziness or is suffering from exhaustion or depression, the cause is often thought to be witchcraft. That is why many people in the rural areas of South America still consult a traditional healer first, because the modern doctor with his university education has no cure for such disorders.

Or there again, many people in the Third World simply have no contact with western medicine and its modern facilities and therefore have no choice but to rely on the old healing methods. But in any case a good many drugs that form part of standard medical practice in the west are derived from plant extracts that have long been found in the repertoire of the shamans: Curare is now a standard narcotic in modern medicine and cardiac surgery, while quinine is used to treat malaria. The leaves of the coca shrub provide a local anaesthetic, and the Indians were using contraceptives long before the 'pill' came on the market in Europe.

The social and cultural background is also of great importance, of course, as it determines the relationship between healer and patient, sickness and health. To the Indians, with their magical beliefs, illness is always based on a disharmony between men, the environment and the cosmos. And it is only by observing certain curative rites that the state of equilibrium can be restored and the discord in the patient's body resolved. The treatment gives the patient fresh vigour, strengthens the bonds between his group and himself and generally mobilises his spiritual strength.

181 Abraham Calazacon is headman of the Colorado Indians and also Ecuador's most famous sorcerer and healer.

182 Abraham has his practice in his jungle house. His patients include Indians, mestizos and whites from all classes of society.
Bottom: On the table he has placed stones, pre-Columbian finds and eggs, which are thought to have magical properties.

183 Throughout the Andean region a ritual form of healing ceremony with eggs, called *limpia de huevo*, is widespread. The therapy involves rubbing the patient's body with eggs so that the disease can be transferred from the body to the eggs.

184–187 This sequence shows the various stages in the healing ritual. The *yachag taita* sprays the egg with brandy as a form of consecration and massages the patient's body with it. The egg is then applied to various parts of the body to suck out the disease.

188 To keep illness away from their houses, the Cayapa Indians set up guard figures made of wood. These guardians are dressed in the uniform of the army of Ecuador in the Thirties, an interesting example of acculturative Indian art.

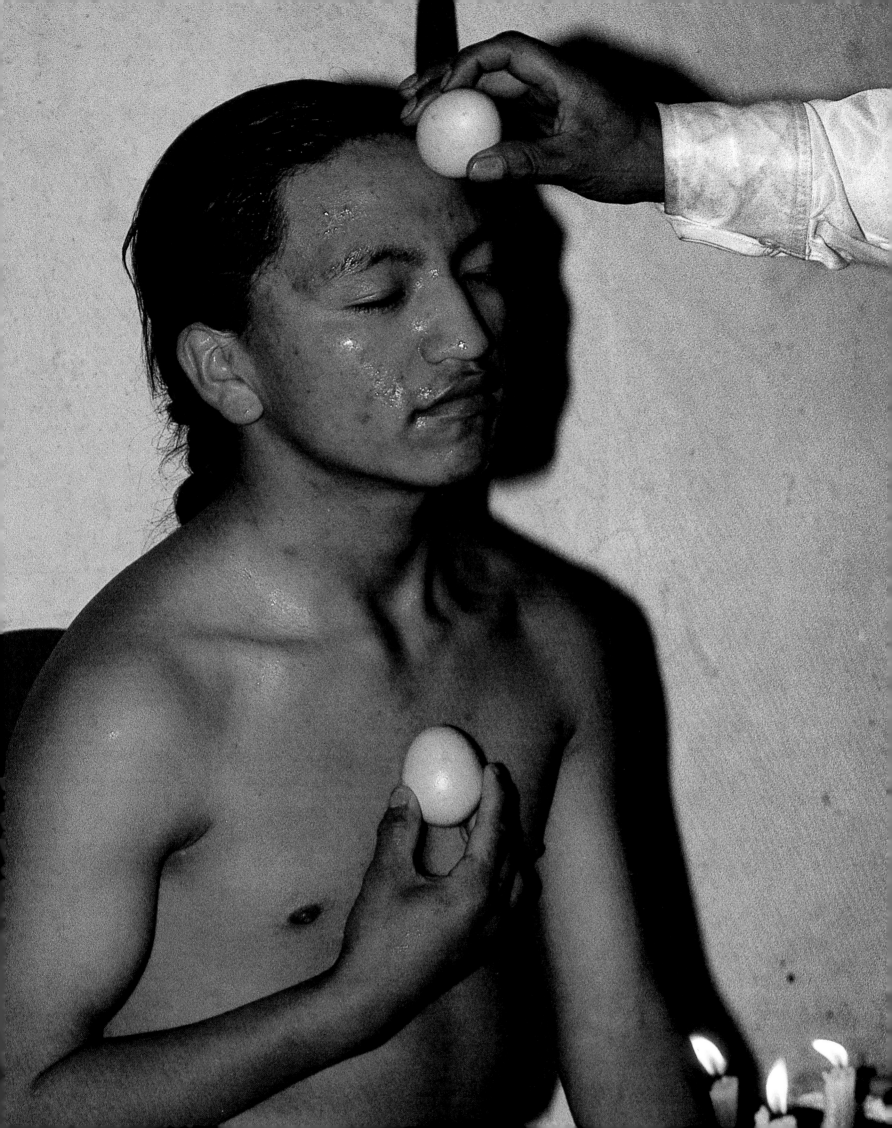

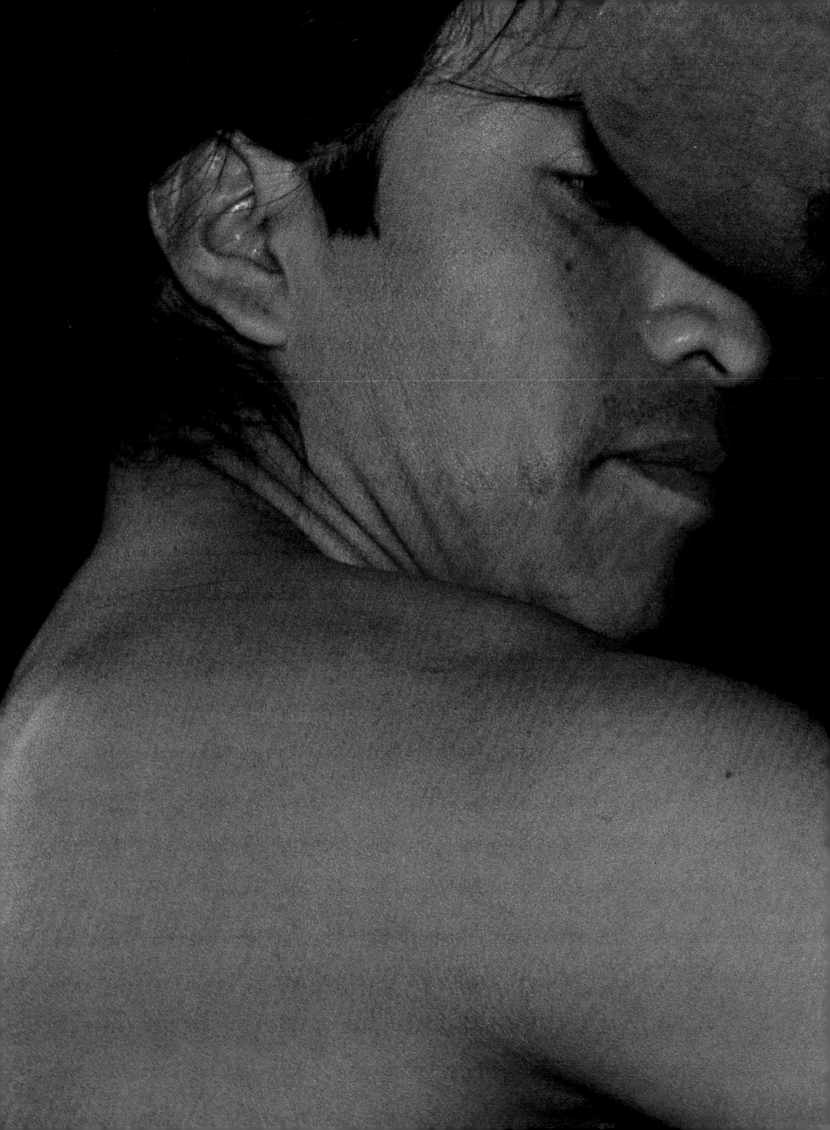

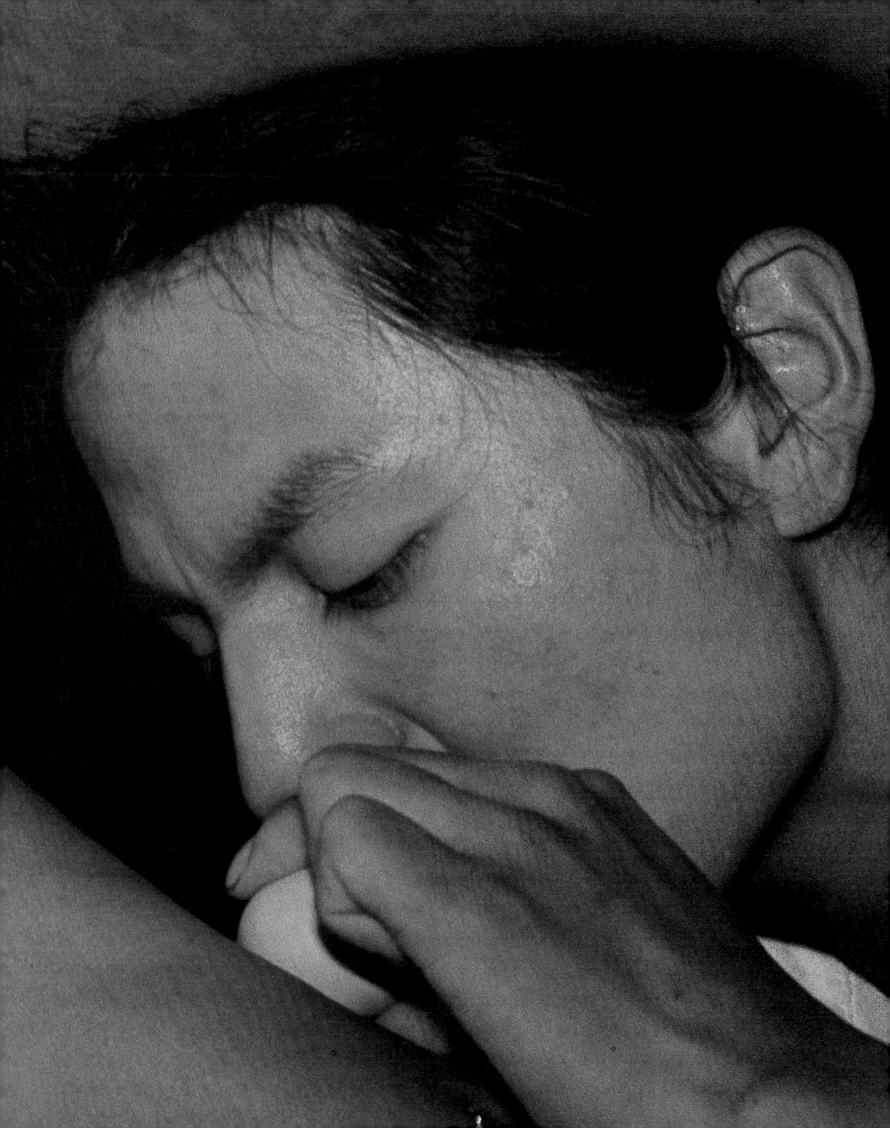

The healing ceremonies themselves are not unlike the modern forms of psychotherapy. Apart from the magical component, treatment also includes herbs, massage and, where necessary, minor surgery.

Given the fact that there will always be a few charlatans and quacks, the serious application of these healing techniques has been presented in a very positive light in recent scientific research. And the World Health Organisation (WHO) of the United Nations has defined its policy in this respect accordingly. Anyone in the Third World who uses ritual methods involving the use of vegetable or animal agents to cure disease can be recognised as a naturopath providing he or she enjoys the confidence of the local people.

The sorcerers and healers we wish to concentrate on here are called *brujos* or *curanderos* in Spanish. They are a type of priest, commanding great esteem and respect in Indian society.

The Indians who live in the villages located round the extinct volcano Imbabura, the sacred mountain of the Otavaleños in the north of the Andean region of Ecuador, have a number of different kinds of ritual healers. Every *comunidad* will have at least one *yachag taita*, a 'man of knowledge', who can heal the sick. They are also known as *hierbatero* (herbalist) or simply as *médico* (doctor).

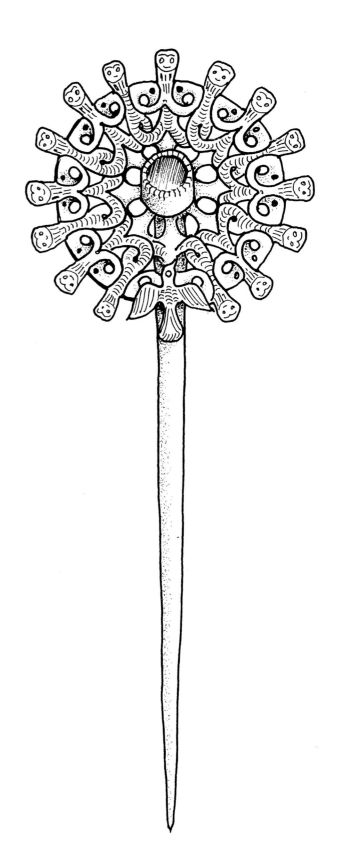

The so called *brujos maleros* or *hechiceros* form a distinct group of their own; for they are the black magicians whose spells can bring harm and suffering to other people. Often, however, the functions of white and black magic, of *curandero* and *brujo,* are combined in one and the same person.

The Quichua of this region distinguish between illness with a 'natural' cause, which can be treated by western doctors, and psychosomatic disorders, which are interpreted in the framework of the tribe's religious and magical beliefs and can only be treated by the local *curandero.* Disorders of this second type can result from the loss of the patient's soul, the introduction of magic objects into his body, or possession by an evil spirit *(supay, diablo).* People are especially at risk through the 'evil eye' *(mal ojo),* which is one reason why they are often unwilling to be photographed.

Even the gusts of wind from the snow-capped peaks of the Andes can be carriers of mischief. One illness that is greatly feared is called *susto,* which means 'fright'. The symptoms are vomiting, diarrhoea and profuse perspiration. The Indians believe that this disease, which is endemic to the Andean tribes, always strikes when some social or religious taboo has been broken. Another disorder, called *mal viento* or *mal aire* is a kind of air sickness with symptoms involving epileptic attacks, hysteria and a state of acute anxiety. In all such cases the patient consults *yachag taita,* who is often a woman.

The healer's aids, apart from his *mesa,* that is the altar itself, comprise his many magic objects, or *poderosos artes.* These ritual objects can be of animal, vegetable or mineral origin. They include stones, pre-Columbian finds, herbs, eggs, animals etc. and symbolise the natural forces. Frequently the *mesa* is also adorned with crosses, or pictures and statues of Catholic saints.

Limpia – the ritual of healing and purification

The actual healing rites are called *limpia,* that is 'purification'. They are based on the belief that evil can be removed from one body and transferred to another. The Indians nowadays assume that the process is effected by electro-magnetic forces found in chicken's eggs, guinea pigs, metal, volcanic rock and in certain other natural elements.

There are various ways of performing a *limpia* or healing ceremony. In the province of Imbabura, the home of the Otavaleños, *limpia de cuy,* or treatment with a guinea pig, is practised. From ethno-historical sources it is known that this method was employed before the Inca

190

period. In his healing rites, *yachag taita* performs diagnosis and therapy in one. He ascertains the nature of the illness and performs the actions that will combat the evil at the same time.

The healing ceremony always takes place in a similar setting and follows the same standard pattern:

1. First the healer decides on the possible causes of the disorder. For this purpose he invokes the spirits of his ancestors, the *gentiles,* and also Catholic saints, to help him in his work.

2. During the ritual, consecration is of the greatest importance. The healer breathes tobacco smoke on the patient, who should be naked where possible, the ceremonial paraphernalia on the altar, and on the guinea pig and then sprays them with a mouthful of *guarapo,* a kind of fermented brandy made from sugercane.

3. Then the *limpia* itself can begin. *Yachag taita* grasps the guinea pig by the neck and rubs it along the patient's body until it suffocates.

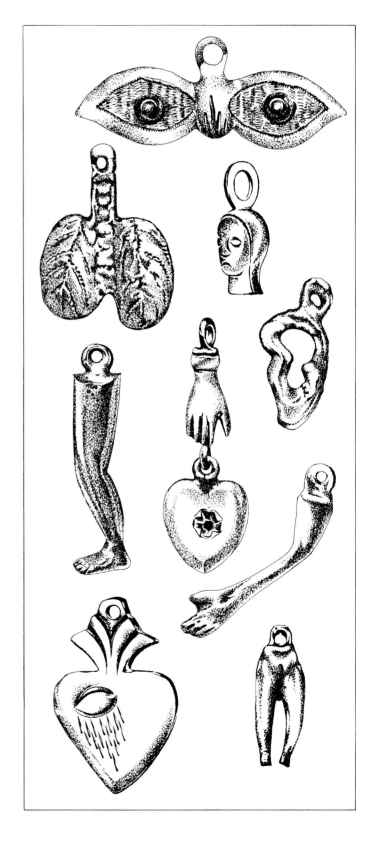

Right: A variety of concrete motifs worked in silver, nickel or lead are common in the Andean region. As an amulet or votive offering, they provide magical protection for the person wearing them or represent an identification sacrifice. Their efficacy is based on the principle of analogy, implying an inner relationship between the figure and its inner meaning. These forms are based on European models. (Drawing: H. W. Jungreuthmayer.)

4. In order to ascertain the severity of the disease, the healer then tears open the guinea pig's skin with his finger nails and begins with his autopsy. From the state and position of the animal's organs the healer can form an opinion of the condition of the patient. This is diagnosis by analogy, with the affected organs in the dead guinea pig corresponding to the focus of the disease in the patient–like effects from like causes. In this symbolical operation, then, the patient's disease is transferred to the animal. On the other hand, the result of this haruspication may be that the patient cannot be cured of his sufferings and must die. When the healing ceremony is over, the dead guinea pig is burried in the ground.

The method with the chicken egg is similar. In this case the patient's body is massaged with the egg, the aim being to transfer the illness from the patient to the egg. After every massage, the egg is broken open, and *yachag taita* performs his divination. A dark yolk is a sign that the evil has been successfully transferred to the egg.

The massages are continued until the colour of the yolk no longer changes. That is interpreted as an indication that the disease has been wholly transferred and that harmony has been restored between the patient and the transcendental forces of the cosmos.

193 A healing ceremony in Iluman, the village of the sorcerers in northern Ecuador. The Quichua healers enjoy great social standing and are thought to have magico-religious powers. The patient is holding a lance made of chonta wood to ward off evil spirits. The *yachag taita* uses two horse-shoes, to which electro-magnetic properties are ascribed, to attract the disease out of the patient's body.

194/195 A regular feature of the healing ritual is the consecration of the patient with sugar-cane brandy. The sorcerer spits a mouthful of this *guarapo* into the patient's face to facilitate the transference of his powers.

196/197 One of the oldest healing processes in the Andes is the *limpia de cuy*, literally 'purification with the guinea-pig'. Here the body of an old woman is massaged with a guinea-pig in order to transfer her illness to the animal. Every now and then the healer consecrates the patient with tobacco smoke.

198/199 The guinea-pig treatment is continued until the animal suffocates. Thereupon the healer tears the animal open and carries out an autopsy as a basis for his diagnosis. The condition of the animal's entrails is a guide to the nature of the patient's disease.

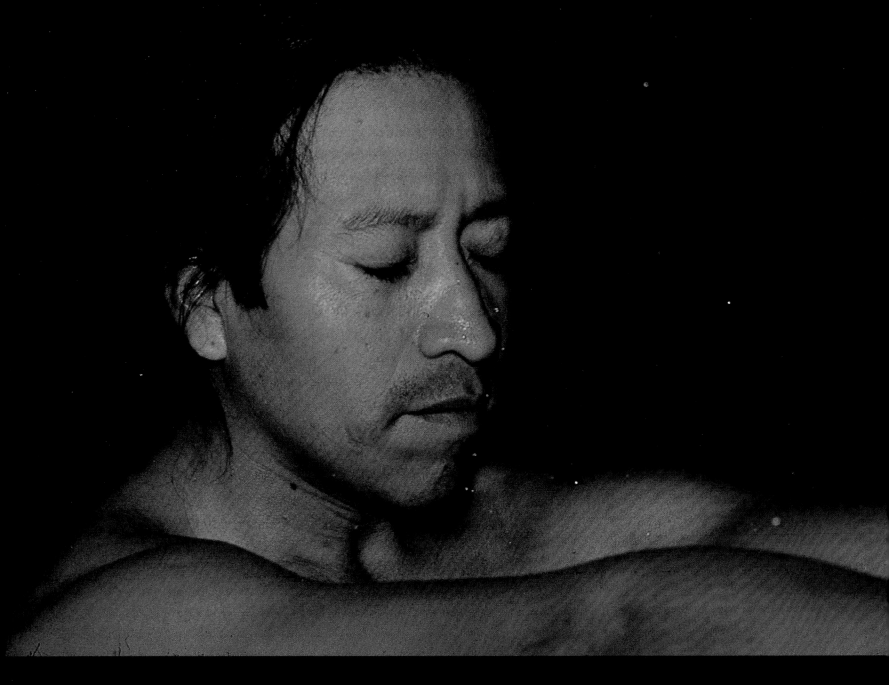

The Chocó

Unlike the indigenous tribes of Africa and Oceania, the Indians of South America have not on the whole produced much in the way of cult statues or figurines in wood. The one big exception is the Chocó tribe, who, together with their neighbours, the Cayapa in Ecuador and the Cuna in Panama, can look back on a fruitful tradition of wood carving.

Their sacral sculptures, statues and also paintings have a natural charm that is very hard to resist. In view of their simple beauty and aesthetic strength, a western observer would normally view these ritual objects as works of art, but in the eyes of their creators they are a form of magical and religious expression that creates the link between the material and the transcendental world. It is only with the help of these cult objects that the shamans can invoke the spirits so as to heal the rich and ward off danger.

The Chocó, who can be divided into two distinct ethno-linguistic subgroups, the Noanamá and the Emberá, differ in many respects from the Indians of the Amazonian lowlands. Their area of settlement is the jungle-covered river deltas on the Pacific coast between the Isthmus of Panama and north-east Colombia.

Their habitat has one of the highest rainfalls on the whole subcontinent of South America. Only rarely does the sun manage to penetrate the darkly laden and depressing sky. Considerable tracts of this region are now inhabited by negroes, who drove the aboriginal people into the remote and inhospitable areas of the small tributaries.

The Chocó, who now number about 5,000, build settlements consisting of individual houses. In the last few years increased contact with the outside world has prompted many Chocó to form whole villages or co-operatives. The traditional Chocó house is a kind of round pile-dwelling without walls, and a typical feature of their architecture is the steep conical roof crowned by an anthropoid ceramic figure at the apex.

The economic base of the Chocó takes the form of plantations, which are frequently affected by flooding. Unlike the other Indian tribes of the South American lowlands, the Chocó do not burn the trees felled to form a clearing, but simply leave them to rot. They cultivate various sorts of maize, manioc and plantain. To enrich their basic diet the Chocó also go hunting and fishing to a limited extent, using shotguns or bows and arrows to kill the game animals and their blow-guns to shoot birds. The darts for their blow-guns are tipped with a poison derived from a certain species of frog.

Although the Chocó Indians are frequent visitors to the ports on the Pacific coast, travelling long distances in their dugouts to get there, one aspect of their culture has survived down to the present time, namely shamanism and their rites and beliefs connected with it.

Ancestors in wood

Their religious traditions concentrate primarily on the spirits of their ancestors, who are responsible for the weal and woe of the people. These supernatural beings are represented by figurines carved in wood, which they call *hai*. Their efficacy is based on the magic powers deriving from a tutelary spirit. It is up to every family and every individual to seek their own *hai*. The spirits of their forebears appear to the Chocó in a dream or state of trance; and they can also appear in a variety of shapes in the jungle, by the river or even in their houses. When still very small, the Chocó children are given little wooden figures, just to play with at first, by the shaman, whom the Chocó call *haibana*. After puberty every Chocó can acquire his or her tutelary spirit with the assistance of the *haibana*. This requires the observance of certain rites, however. First of all, the adults who are seeking their tutelary spirits move into a small jungle hut with the shaman and spend their time there carving simple figures of wood. By fasting, staying awake or taking hallucinogenic drugs, they try to induce a visionary state, in which their tutelary spirits will appear to them. The *haibana* helps them by telling them what sacrifices the spirit demands. Normally the price of the spirit's future assistance is charcoal, which is placed in front of the figurine, or human blood, which the *hai* imbibes from a sleeping person in the shape of a vampire. Apart from the visions, a sudden rustling sound or other strange noises announce the presence of these spiritual beings.

In cases of serious illness the magical potency of one's own tutelary spirit will not be sufficient to effect a cure, and one has to turn to the *haibana*, who has a number of magical figurines at his disposal for just this purpose. These are carved with great care from dark and heavy hardwoods and polished to a shine. In length, these ceremonial staffs vary between 15 cm and one metre, with just the upper part carved in the form of an animal or anthropoid figure. As in the case of the Cuna or Cayapa, the external shape of the carvings is not as important as the magic substance that is inherent in the *hai*. In addition to these ceremonial staffs, every shaman has a large number of wooden figurines, which are each used to combat one specific disorder.

The *haibana* of the Chocó have to undergo a long apprenticeship with a master shaman so as to learn the magic rites, the techniques for attaining a visionary state, and also the properties of the various herbs. One of the central aids in the initiation process is the 'spirit boat'. The novice who is aspiring to magical powers first carves a canoe-shaped boat and several small figures out of balsa-wood. The master shaman than places the boat and crew on the roof of his house and sits the budding magician directly underneath it. Then the *haibana* and his pupil invoke the spirits of their ancestors. If certain rhythmic sounds are heard in the course of the ritual, it means that the *hai* are having sexual intercourse with the wooden figurines. And that is a sign that the anthropomorphous figures have received the powers of the ancestral spirits.

On the Río Tuira, in the jungles of Darien that cover the isthmus joining Panama and Colombia, I once had the opportunity to attend a healing ceremony. A boy of about eleven, shaking with bouts of fever, was brought to a well-known shaman for

203

A ceremonial staff of dark hardwood with a carefully polished carving and an old sabre are the shaman's vehicles of communication with the Indians' ancestral spirits. The carving at the top of the ceremonial staff represents a monkey wearing a western-style hat. The carved figure is seen as the permanent home of the shaman's tutelary spirit, while the sabre is only temporarily invested with magical powers. Integrating foreign elements into their traditional culture is an expression and component of Indian emancipation and self-reliance.

treatment. The patient was laid on his back on a platform in the house of the *haibana.* There then followed a truly remarkable ceremony. First, the shaman took a bundle of carved narrow strips of balsa-wood, which he keeps concealed in his house. One side of these wooden strips is decorated with geometrical patterns painted in red and blue, while the most striking feature is a face carved in relief in the top third of the design. Using these wooden strips, the *haibana* then formed a kind of roof structure which he placed over the patient's body, leaving his head and feet protruding at either end. Then the shaman sat by the patient's head and took a short ceremonial staff, which he used to summon the spirits in a monotonous incantation to transfer their magic powers to the patient and remove the spiritual projectiles from his body. The purpose of the roof-like construction with the carved strips of balsa was to create a magical zone in which the tutelary spirits can more easily concentrate their powers on the patient.

The *hai,* which play such an important part in the lives of the Chocó, represent as it were their wishes to the spirits of their ancestors, which can bring fertility and drive out disease. Equally, however, they have a regulatory function in the social lives of the Chocó, since infringements of their social norms can also turn the *hai* into a danger to man.

200   A Chocó shaman or *haibana* uses his *hai,* that is his ritual staffs carved in wood, to summon the ancestral spirits.

205   The densely forested flats of the rivers are thought to be the home of supernatural forces.

206/207   A healing ritual on the Río Tuira. The shaman kneels by the head of the patient lying under a tent of carved and painted balsa-wood boards. With the assistance of his *hai* and a large number of incantations, the shaman then attempts to drive out the disease.

208/209   The recognised shamans receive a steady stream of patients every day. Here a *haibana* is using bunches of magic plants to concentrate the disease at one point in the patient's body so that he can suck it out.

210/211   Two girls have painted themselves with a dark-blue dye *(jagua)* to protect themselves from evil. Their silver jewellery made of silver coins from Colombia or Panama is a typical feature of the Chocó.

The Guajiro

The Guajiro Indians live on the semi-desert Guajira Peninsula in the extreme north of the subcontinent of South America. Most of the peninsula belongs to Colombia, although a narrow coastal strip in the east is Venezuelan territory. The local topography, intense sunshine, strong winds and long periods of drought combine to create a landscape dominated by the thornbush and cactus. Only for a short period of the year, from September to December, do torrential rains set in and tornadoes sweep the area, transforming the Guajira into one vast morass. In a region that is so different from the rest of South America over 100,000 Guajiro Indians, or, in their own tongue, Wayú, have their home. Their language belongs to the linguistic family of the Arawaks, who inhabited large stretches of the West Indies and the South American subcontinent in the pre-Columbian era. Today the Guajiro comprise the biggest Indian population in the South American lowlands. Only in the Andean areas have still bigger autochthonous groups managed to survive.

In the course of their history the Guajiro have always succeeded in adapting to changing conditions. At the very beginning of the colonial era they took over cattle-breeding from the whites, a move that has since proved decisive for their culture. This is in fact the only example where an Indian people has abandoned its traditional economic base of hunting and horticulture in favour of a semi-nomadic existence as stock-farmers.

Needless to say, this acculturation was not the result of a sudden decision but rather of a process that covered several generations. In order to acquire cattle, sheep, goats, donkeys and horses, the Guajiro went pearl-diving in the Caribbean, using their harvest to barter with the Spaniards. They were also fortunate in that their land was so dry and barren and their manner so warlike that the Conquistadors had little desire to seize their territory.

Cattle now play a predominant role in the lives of this ethnic group. The transformation from a tribe of hunters to semi-nomadic herdsmen did of course involve extensive adjustments to their system of social and religious values. The animals are kept as personal property and can be acquired by women as well as men. Although sheep and goats are the most widespread of their animals, cattle are the greatest status symbol and are an expression of social prestige and economic power. The importance attached to the cattle is reflected in the fact that sick animals are treated by a shaman in a special ritual ceremony.

Stock-owning is closely connected with the social structure of the Guajiro tribe. The cattle are viewed as members of the family group and are branded with the clan symbol. This sense of identification with their cattle goes so far that cattle-stealing is punished just as severely as wife-snatching. Also, the members of the family are not allowed to eat the meat of their own cattle, as that would be an almost incestuous act.

The *casta* system

Guajiro society is composed of *castas*, that is sibs or clans, which are based on the maternal line. In this social system, the children of a family group belong to the mother's family, and their maternal uncle is responsible for their education and their inheritance. At the age of nine, the boys go to live with their uncle, and from then on they are considered members of the *e'iruku*, which means 'flesh rel-atives', while the relatives of the boy's father are called 'blood relatives'.

It is estimated that there are about 30 *castas* scattered throughout the tribal territory, which are divided into further subgroups. Each *casta* is ruled by a *cazique* or headman, who represents the group's interests and has a great deal of political power. Men of great social prestige usually have several wives, although marriage within the *casta* is not permitted.

Guajiro society is based on hierarchical principles. By virtue of their larger stock of cattle, some clans are considered to be richer and have more influence than others, who are thought to be poor and of little account. The members of a *casta* consider themselves related to each other, because they are all descended from a common mythological forebear, who is associated with a certain animal.

This complicated and ramified system of family ties was of great advantage to me for my journeys through Guajiro territory. The interior of the peninsula in particular, which is hardly policed in any way, is in fact one of the most dangerous places in South America, because the Colombian cocaine rings operate their drug smuggling activities from there. For a visitor, therefore, the patronage of a *cazique* and his *casta* is the best assurance available of being able to return home safely with one's expensive cameras and equipment.

Driving through the Guajira, one frequently sees herdsmen wandering across the barren plains with their sheep, goats, cattle, donkeys and horses, searching for a waterhole and pasture. It is the lack of water that keeps the Guajiro Indians constantly on the move, although they have a system of wells, recently equipped with wind-driven pumping systems, to provide them with this *sine qua non* for life itself. The belongings of these Indians are designed exclusively for their semi-nomadic existence. Their total household property is likely to comprise simple windbreaks, which serve them as a home on their wanderings, hammocks for sitting in, relaxing and sleeping, gourds, earthenware vessels, and beautifully crocheted carriers for their beasts of burden.

A cactus to live in

During the rainy season the Guajiro Indians move into permanent settlements, which may comprise up to fifty houses within a stone's throw of each other. The sign of the territorial unit of a *casta* is the cemetery, where they keep the clan's burial urns.

The houses themselves are unique, being constructed around a wooden framework, called *yotojoro,* which is actually the skeleton of a giant cactus. The gable roof is covered with palm-leaves or split cactus bark, and two forked tree-trunks at either end give the house the necessary stability. The kitchen is built separate from the living quarters, and a remarkable construction it is, comprising a circular hedge of giant cactus. Nowadays, there is a tendency to use dried clay brick instead of cactus wood. Sometimes the houses, or even the whole settlement, are surrounded by a palisade of cactus as a protection against possible attack.

The diet of these Indians is based on milk and cheese, with meat reserved for ceremonial occasions. The Guajiro also buy a lot of their food at the markets held regularly in Riohacha, Maicao and Paraguaypoa. A major source of income is the sale of cattle and also the manufacture of hammocks, while smuggling between Colombia and Venezuela is a thriving industry. Hunting, and fishing along the coast, especially for turtle, are very much a minor activity nowadays. Although hunting with shotguns or bows and arrows is still a source of social prestige for the men, it can now be viewed as a relic of the time before stockfarming was introduced. They also have an interesting piece of hunting equipment for hunting rabbits, namely a kind of throwing stick, which in this form is unique in South America.

In some parts of the Guajira, salt and gypsum are mined. After the rainy season, several hundred men and women assemble at the sites along the coast to spend a few weeks digging for salt and collecting the gypsum that has formed through evaporation.

Today the oil towns and industrial centres on Lake Maracaibo in Venezuela have a magnetic attraction for many Guajiro, and Zurima, a suburb of Maracaibo, already houses more than 20,000 Indians. They can be seen everywhere, at the markets, in the towns on the fringe of the Guajira, and in the buses, easily identifiable by their national dress, which they still continue to wear in spite of their contacts with the world of the *alejunas,* the whites. Traditional Guajiro dress for men is the *taparro,* a loincloth that is held in place by means of a woven belt. The fastener is of crochet work or brightly coloured tassles. In the meantime the men have also taken to sombreros, sun glasses and Japanese shirts.

Tu' uma and old gold jewellery

The women wear long flowing cotton dresses shaped like a sack. They are called *manta* and now represent both national dress and an excellent export article. But a Guajiro woman's most prized possession is a necklace made of semi-precious stones, called *tu' uma,* often interspersed with gold beads. The latter are

212   A *cazique* riding on a mule, the foremost beast of burden in the desert-like Guajira.

217   Women enjoy high standing in the matriarchal society of the Guajiro.

218/219   A herd of animals at a water-hole in Alta Guajira. The Guajiro learnt stock-farming from the Spaniards 400 years ago, and today cattle, sheep and goats form the economic base of these Indians.

220   Top: In the dry period donkeys are used to drag the water to the settlements in barrels or steel drums. Bottom: A cactus house in northern Guajira.

221   A Guajiro woman in her traditional *manta* sitting in front of her house.

222   At secondary burial, the remains of the deceased are buried in funeral urns.

223   The function of the skulls is to ward off the *yoluja,* the souls of the dead.

224   A Guajiro has slaughtered a goat. Meat is only eaten on special occasions.

216

sometimes decorated with animal designs, including turtles, frogs or birds, and are thought to go back to the pre-Columbian Tairona culture. The *tu' uma* stones are handed down from mother to daughter. A fine specimen might cost several dozen head of cattle and is a highly prized marriage present.

The women paint their faces with black, brown or yellow pigments made from plant extracts mixed with goat's fat. The various motifs they use are not just an aesthetic exercise but also protect the women's faces from the glare of the tropical sun.

Spirits and double burial

Although most Guajiro Indians are members of the Catholic Church, many of the beliefs and concepts of their old Indian religion still linger on, revolving mainly around the function of the shaman or *piache*, who acts as an intermediary between man and his gods. Dreams are very important to the Guajiro; everyone can have them, of course, but only the *piache* can understand and interpret them. The most important supernatural beings are the *wanuru*, the spirits of the dead. The shaman can make contact with them and ask for advice.

The funeral rites of the Guajiro are also unusual. When one of their number dies, the 'primary funeral' is held. This means that the body is actually buried in a coffin to the accompaniment of ceremonial tears shed by the relatives. In memory of the deceased, the funeral guests are presented with a whole animal, which they must eat at home.

Then, after a space of two or three years, the skeleton of the deceased is disinterred and a new ceremony held. Again the dead Guajiro is made the subject of ritualised mourning, and large quantities of a sugar-cane brandy called *chirinchi* are drunk in his honour. The Guajiro believe that in the meantime his *yoluja,* or soul, will have departed to the world beyond, where it will live a life similar to that on earth. The central aspect of the ceremony can now follow: the 'secondary burial'. First the remaining bones are cleaned by a female relative before being placed in an earthenware urn. This is then stored in the cemetery of the *casta*. Once this second ceremony has been completed, the Guajiro's mortal remains are quietly forgotten.

Although many traditional aspects of their culture have already disappeared, the Guajiro's unswerving commitment to the clan structure has enabled them to preserve their ethnic identity. It is to be hoped that this self-assured people will continue to be successful in meeting new challenges with their own resources, as they have done in the past.

225

ligious community flew sorties over the Auca villages, dropping 'presents'. Then they fixed loudspeakers to the wings of the aircraft and bombarded them with promises and biblical quotations in the Auca language. And after a time they succeeded in evacuating 500 Auca from the tribal region and taking them to a reservation of about 400 acres total area.

The Auca who once lived on the meat of monkeys, on larvae and berries, are now dependent on the white man, working as day labourers and spending their hard-earned money on things they had found for nothing or did not need. But now their system of values is characterised by imported canned food, transistor radios and guns. Their hair, once groomed with care and worn with pride, is now cropped short with a pair of old scissors. That way, it is not 'savage' any more. Their ear plugs are missing, leaving the stretched lobes to flap unaesthetically around their necks. And for clothes they now wear faded shirts and ill-fitting shorts courtesy of the USA, and often enough woollen socks, baseball caps and sloppy old sneakers. Men and women who were used to walking around naked only 50 miles away now bathe in the river fully clothed. They have learnt to be ashamed of their unspoilt nature.

But even the Auca living in self-imposed jungle isolation on the Río Cononaco cannot expect to live undisturbed for much longer. In 1979, when we wanted to pay them a visit, we found that the landing strip once laid out by an oil company and since abandoned had been blocked with oil drums. Only when Samuel Padilla, whose mother is a Huaorani, dropped a basket woven by that group of Indians as a recognition signal did they remove the barrier. But, also in 1979, white visitors introduced influenza to the area, which led to the death of two children. The children's father could not understand what had happened, presumed it was the result of an evil spell, and slew his neighbour. And there are other problems, too, such as an acute shortage of partners for marriage. The two groups that still live in isolation are now so small that it is almost impossible for them to observe the strict rules of exogamy to which any marriage is subject. Consequently, a girl who wishes to marry must leave the jungle behind her.

But in any case it is only a matter of time now before the bulldozers, drilling rigs and construction gangs arrive in the jungle of the Cononaco, which will then become the former hunting grounds of the last of the Auca. Then Mengha, Tita and Nape will lay aside their blow-guns and take up the spade to build another helipad. And the world will have lost out on another of its people and another piece of its history.

253

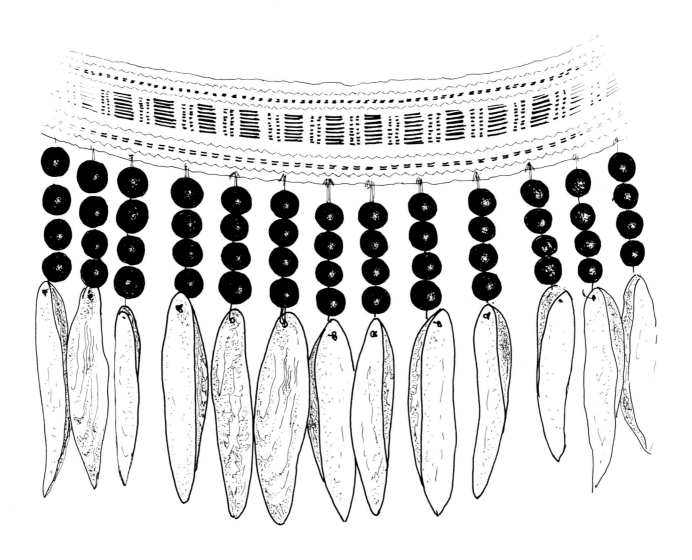

Appendix

Glossary

achiote	An orange-red dye from the pulp of a Central American fruit
arutam	A kind of vision or spiritual image (Jivaro)
ayahuasca	A hallucinogenic beverage prepared from certain liana plants and known by a variety of names in Amazonia
brujo	Magician, medicine-man, shaman (Spanish)
chagra	A plantation cleared from the tropical forest of the lowlands
chicha	A fermented beverage prepared from manioc, fruits or corn of varying alcoholic strength
chirinchi	The sugar-cane brandy of the Guajiro
cholo	A half-caste in the Andean region, often derogatory
curandero	Healer (Spanish)
cuy	Guinea-pig
dabucurí	The ceremonial gatherings of the Tukano
ebena	See *yopo*
FUNAI	Fundacão Nacional aos Indios, the National Indian Foundation in Brazil
guarapo	Sugar-cane brandy
hacienda	Landed estate (Spanish)
haibana	A Chocó shaman
huasipunguero	Day-labourer
Indio	Derogatory term for an Indian in South America
indígena	Latin-American word for an Indian
kakaram	Mighty warrior or head-hunter of the Jivaro
maloca	Communal house in north-west Amazonia
mestizo	A half-caste offspring of a European and an Indian
onoto	See *anatta*
payé	A Tukano shaman
shaboliwa	A Yanomami shaman
shabono	A traditional Yanomami house
sertanista	An expert on Indian affairs at FUNAI
SPI	Serviçao de Proteção aos Indios, the former Indian protection agency in Brazil
tsantsa	Shrunken head
tsetsak	The shamans' magic arrows
yachag taita	A sorcerer and healer in the Andes
yagé	See *ayahuasca*
yopo	Narcotic snuff
yuruparí	Ceremonial rites of the Indians in north-west Amazonia

The pronunciation of Spanish words in Latin America

c   before e and i is pronounced like a voiceless s (e.g. 'sit').
ch   is pronounced as in the English word 'church'.
h   is mute.
j   is pronounced like ch in Scottish 'loch'.
ll   is pronounced like y in 'yellow'.
qu   is pronounced like k in 'kick'.

s
z } are pronounced like a voiceless s (e.g. 'sit').

Notes on the drawings

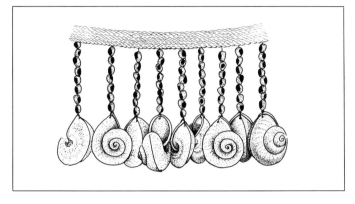

2 A Jivaro woman's dancing belt. It comprises a metre length of cotton braiding with 37 snail shells, each fastened with a cord of palm fibre decorated with seeds.

35 Rock carving from the jungle of southern Venezuela. The petroglyph has been interpreted as a symbol of the sun.

80 An 'x-ray' rock carving from Caicara in Venezuela, thought to represent a jaguar.

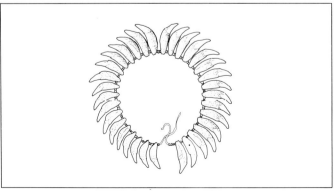

182 A medicine-man's neck ornament with thirty-three jaguar teeth threaded together with small beads, Siona, Río Aguarico, Ecuador.

132 *Mucahua.* A Canelo drinking vessel for *chicha* in multi-coloured earthenware, from the Río Curaray, Ecuador.

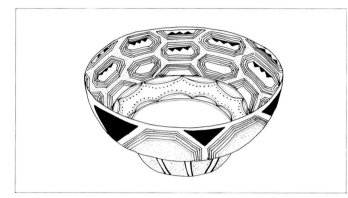

178 A Quichua woman's silver brooch *(tupo)*, 14 cm in diameter, from Imbabura Province, Ecuador.

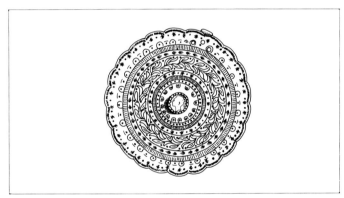

189 A silver-plated nickel brooch *(tupo)* of the Saraguro Indians in the southern Andean region of Ecuador. The disc with the heads represents the sun. Length 20 cm.

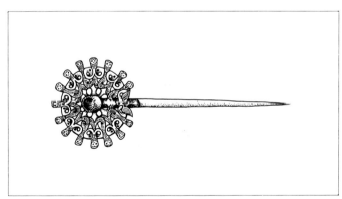

254 A Jivaro dancing belt. The metre length of colourful cotton has 26 palm-fibre cords, onto which seeds and the shell of a fresh-water muscle are threaded.

The illustrated artifacts are part of the author's private collection.

CHILE   ARGENTINA

PARAGUAY

Drawing: H.W. Jungreuthmayer

0   200   400 km

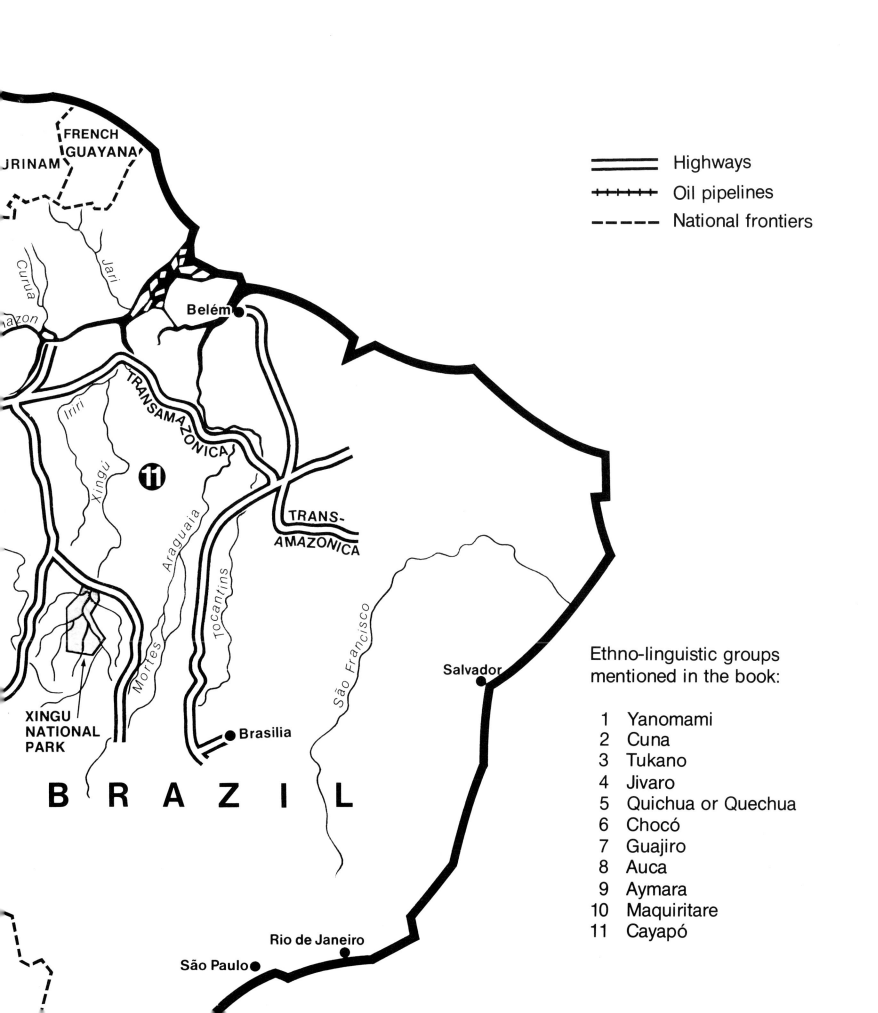

Highways
Oil pipelines
National frontiers

FRENCH
GUAYANA

JRINAM

Curua

Jari

Amazon

Belém

TRANSAMAZONICA

Iriri

Xingú

Araguaia

11

TRANS-
AMAZONICA

Mortes

Tocantins

São Francisco

Salvador

XINGU
NATIONAL
PARK

B R A Z I L

Brasilia

Rio de Janeiro

São Paulo

Ethno-linguistic groups
mentioned in the book:

1   Yanomami
2   Cuna
3   Tukano
4   Jivaro
5   Quichua or Quechua
6   Chocó
7   Guajiro
8   Auca
9   Aymara
10 Maquiritare
11 Cayapó

Bibliography

General

Baumann, P., and Uhlig, H.: *Rettet die Naturvölker, Kein Platz für 'wilde' Menschen,* Safari Verlag, Berlin 1979

Brooks, E., Fuerst, R., Hemming, J., and Huxley, F.: *Tribes of the Amazon Basin in Brazil 1972,* Report for the Aborigines Protection Society, London 1973

Collier, R.: *The River that God Forgot: The Story of the Amazon Rubber Boom,* Dutton, New York 1968

Disselhof, H. D., and Zerries, O.: *Die Erben des Inkareiches und die Indios der Wälder,* Safari Verlag, Berlin 1974

World Council of Churches: *The Situation of the Indians in South America.* Geneva 1972

Eibl-Eibesfeldt, I.: *Menschenforschung auf neuen Wegen. Die naturwissenschaftliche Betrachtung kultureller Verhaltensweisen,* Molden Verlag, Vienna 1976

Friede, J., Friedeman, N., and Fajado, D.: *Indígenismo y Anaquilamento de Indígenas en Colombia,* Bogotá 1975

Lévi-Strauss, C.: *Tristes Tropiques,* Atheneum, New York 1974

Melia, B. S. I.: *Wenn die Kaimane die Schmetterlinge auffressen,* Pogrom, Report Nr. 7, 3–6, Hamburg 1977

Müller-Schneck, J., Dirx, R., and Schulz, U.: *Indianische Hoffnungen,* Jugenddienst Verlag, Wuppertal 1979

Rivera, J. E.: *La Vorágine,* Bogotá 1924

Ribeiro, D.: *Fronteras Indígenas de la Civilización,* Siglo Veintiuno Editores, Mexico 1973

–: *Unterentwicklung, Kultur und Zivilisation. Ungewöhnliche Versuche,* Suhrkamp, Frankfurt 1980

Schultes, R. E., and Hofman, A.: *Plants of the Gods,* Hutchinson, London 1979

Trupp, F., Haller, F., and Pereira, J. L.: *Indígenas Olvidados. Cambio Cultural en el Oriente Ecuatoriano,* 16-mm-Film, Universidad Católica, Quito 1977

Varese, St.: *The Forest Indians in the Present Political Situation of Peru,* IWGIA Document, Copenhagen 1972

Wilbert, J.: *Survivors of Eldorado,* Praeger, New York 1972

The Yanomami

Barandiarán, D., Brändli, B., and Walalam, A.: *Los Hijos de la Luna,* Caracas 1974

Biocca, E.: *Mondo Yanoama,* Ed. Leonardo da Vinci, Bari 1965

–: *Ein weißes Mädchen in der Urwaldhölle,* Ullstein, Frankfurt 1972

Chagnon, N.: *Yanomami. The Fierce People,* Holt, Rinehart and Winston, New York 1972

Cocco, L.: *Iyewei-teri, Quince Años entre los Yanomami,* Escuela Tecnica Popular Don Bosco Boleíta, Caracas 1972

Lizot, J.: *Le Cercle des Feaux. Faits et Dits des Indiens Yanomami,* Recherches anthropol. au Seuil, Paris 1976

Steinvorth Goetz, I.: *Uriji jami! Life and Belief of the Forest Waika on the Upper Orinoco,* Asociación Cultural Humboldt, Caracas 1970

Zerries, O.: *Waika. Die kulturgeschichtliche Stellung der Waika-Indianer des Oberen Orinoco im Rahmen der Völkerkunde Südamerikas,* Klaus Renner Verlag, Munich 1964

–, and Schuster, M.: *Mahekodeti. Monographie eines Dorfes der Waika-Indianer (Yanoama) am oberen Orinoko,* Klaus Renner Verlag, Munich 1974

The Cuna

Hartmann, G.: *Molakana. Volkskunst der Cuna, Panama,* catalogue, Museum für Völkerkunde, Berlin 1980

Keeler, C.: *Cuna Indian Art: The Art and Craft of Panama's San Blas Islands,* New York 1969

Nordenskiöld, E.: *A Historical and Ethnological Survey of the Cuna Indians,* Comparative Ethnographical Studies, Vol. 10, Göteborg 1938

Rautenstrauch-Joest-Museum: *Die San Blas Cuna. Ein Indianerstamm in Panama,* catalogue, Cologne 1977

Stout, D. B.: *San Blas Cuna Acculturation: An Introduction,* Viking Fund Publications in Anthropology, No. 9, New York 1947

Wafer, L.: *A New Voyage and Description of the Isthmus of America,* London 1699 (repr.: Cleveland 1903)

Ghosts of Granite

Carvajal, J.: *L'Art rupèstre en Colombie,* Style, No. 2, 58–67, Lausanne 1962

Reichel-Dolmatoff, G.: *Rock-Paintings of the Vaupés: An Essay of Interpretation,* Folklore Americas, No. 26, 107–113, Los Angeles 1967

Sujo Volsky, J.: *El Estudio del Arte Rupestre en Venezuela,* Universidad Católica. Caracas 1975

The Tukano

Goldman, I.: *The Cubeo Indians of the Northwest Amazon,* University of Illinois Press, Urbana 1963

Koch-Grünberg, T.: *Zwei Jahre unter den Indianern. Reisen in Nordwest-Brasilien,* 2 Vols., Berlin 1909 to 1910 (reprinted: Graz 1967)

Reichel-Dolmatoff, G.: *Amazonian Cosmos: The Sexual and Religious Symbolism of the Tukano,* University of Chicago Press, Chicago 1971

–: *The Shaman and the Jaguar. A Study of Narcotic Drugs Among the Indians of Colombia,* Temple Philadelphia 1975

Trupp, F.: *Mythen der Makuna,* Acta Ethnologica et Linguistica, No. 40, Vienna 1977

–, and Haller, F.: *Barasana (Südost-Kolumbien, Provinz Vaupés). Rituelles Federschmuckfest bei den Barasana (Yeba-masá),* Film D 1398, IWF Göttingen 1980

Building with Nature

Barandiarán, D.: *El Habitado entre los Indios Yecuana,* Antropológica, No. 16, Caracas 1966

Bola, L., and Róvere, F.: *La Casa Achuar,* Mundo Shuar, Fasciculo No. 9, Quito 1977

Guidoni, E.: *Primitive Architecture,* Abrams, New York 1978

Johnson, R.: *La Casa Achuar y el Ambiente,* Mundo Shuar, Fasciculo No. 8, Quito 1977

Münzel, M.: *Schrumpfkopf-Macher? Jibaro-Indianer in Südamerika,* exhibition catalogue, Museum für Völkerkunde, Frankfurt 1977

Reichel-Dolmatoff, G.: *Amazonian Cosmos,* Chicago 1971

The Jivaro

Chirif, A., and Mora, C.: *Atlas de Comunidades Nativas,* Dirección General de Organización es Rurales, Lima 1977

Directorio de la Federación Shuar: *Federación de Centros Shuar,* Sucua 1976

Harner, M.: *The Jivaro. People of the Sacred Waterfall,* Anchor, New York 1972

Karsten, R.: *The Head-Hunters of Western Amazon. The Life and Culture of the Jibaro Indians of Eastern Ecuador and Peru,* Helsingfors 1935

The Quichua

Collier, J., and Buitron, A.: *The Awakening Valley,* Instituto Otavaleño de Antropología, Quito 1971

Icaza, J.: *Huasipungo,* Buenos Aires 1953 (reprint)

Oberem, U.: *Los Quijos. Historia de la Transculturación de un Grupo Indígena en el Oriente Ecuatoriano,* Madrid 1971

Spahni, J. C.: *Los Indios de Los Andes,* Editorial Piedra Santa, 1979

Whitten, N. E.: *Sacha Runa. Ethnicity and Adaptation of Ecuadorian Jungle Quichua,* University of Illinois Press, Urbana 1976

Sorcerers and Healers

Estrella, E.: *Medicina Aborigen. La Práctica Médica Aborigen de la Sierra Ecuatoriana,* Editorial Epoca, Quito 1977

Hargous, S.: *Beschwörer der Seelen. Das magische Universum südamerikanischer Indianer,* Sphinx Verlag, Basle 1976

The Chocó

Reichel-Dolmatoff, G.: *Contribuciones a la Etnografía de los Indios del Chocó,* Revista Colombiana de Antropología, Vol. XI, Bogotá 1962

Wassen, H.: *Estudios Chocoes,* Etnologisca Studier 26, Göteborg 1963

Zerries, O.: *Holzgeschnitzte Menschen leben. Ein Mythologem und seine kultischen Entsprechungen. Ein Beitrag zum Problem der anthropomorphen Holzschnitzerei im naturvölkischen Südamerika*, Paideuma, Vol. XIX/XX, Wiesbaden 1973

The Guajiro

Baranquilla, J. A.: *Así es La Guajira*, Barranquilla 1946

Perrin, M.: *El Camino de los Indios Muertos, Mitos y Simbolos Guajiros*, Monte Avila Editores, Caracas 1980

Wilbert, J.: *Goajiro Kinship and the Eiruku Cycle*, University of California, Los Angeles 1970

The Auca

Baumann, P., and Patzelt, E.: *Menschen im Regenwald. Expedition Auka*, Droste, Düsseldorf 1975

Blomberg, R.: *The Naked Aucas*, G. Allen and Unwin Ltd., London 1956

Elliot, E.: *The Savage my Kinsman*, Harper & Row, New York 1977

Gartelmann, K.: *El Mundo Perdido de los Aucas*, Quito 1977

Kingsland, M., and Wright, J.: *A Saint Among Savages*, Collins, London 1980

Trupp, F., and Haller, F.: *Tieflandindianer in der 'Erdölkultur'*, Zeitschrift für Lateinamerika, No. 12, 136–149, Vienna 1977

Wallis, E. E.: *Aucas Downriver. Dayuma's Story Today*, Harper and Row, New York 1973

Yost, J.: *El Desarollo Comunitario y la Supervivencia Etnica. El Caso de los Huaorani*, Cuadernos Etnolinguisticos No. 6, Quito 1979

Zerries, O.: *Die kulturgeschichtliche Stellung der Auca unter den Urwaldindianern Südamerikas*, in: Baumann/Patzelt 1975

Acknowledgements

This book is dedicated to my wife Ilse, who has been of inestimable help to me, both in the jungle and at home.

It gives me very great pleasure to thank my Indian hosts in South America, without whose assistance this book could never have been produced.

In addition I should like to offer sincere thanks to my friends, and the authorities and institutions who have helped me in my work and expeditions:

Austrian Consulate General, Quito
Jesus Cierna, Río Vaupés
Hernán Dominguez, La Pederera/C
Federación Shuar, Sucua
Dr Herbert Grubmayr, Austrian Ambassador, Bogotá
Dr Othmar Huber, Austrian Latin America Institute, Vienna
Instituto Colombiano de Antropologiá, Bogotá
Rudolf Lehnhart, Austrian Embassy, Bogotá
Oficina General de la OEA, Quito
Oficina Ministerial de Asuntos Indígenas, Caracas
Ingrid and Joe Ploner, Seewalchen/A, Austria
Pontificia Universidad Católica del Ecuador, Quito
Dr Evi and Dr Wolfgang Ptak
Walter and Gerlinde Zaisberger, Quito

The Valero family, Upper Orinoco
Bernd Wiesner, jungle pilot
Dr Richard Wotava, Austrian Embassy, Caracas

I am also very grateful to Dr Benedikt Erhard of the Perlinger publishing house and Dago Mayr of the Welsermühl printing company for their technical advice and moral support.

All the photographs in this book were taken by the author from 1971 to 1981 with the exception of those on pages 18/19 (H. Schlenker), 230/213 (K. Gartelmann), and 233 and 236 (A. Hirtz). The black-and-white photographs on pages 131, 163, 172, 173, and 174/175 are by I. Trupp.

About half the photographs were taken with Canon F 1, Canon A 1 and Rolleiflex SL 66, while the others were taken with Asahai Pentax 6 × 7, all with a variety of lenses.

The films used were Agfachrome 50 S Professional, Kodachrome 64, Ektachrome 200 and 400, and Kodak Plus X Pan.

Further illustrated volumes published by Perlinger Verlag

Gert Chesi

The Last Africans

240 pages, 148 colour plates, numerous black-and-white photographs and illustrations. 23,5 × 31 cm, cloth bound.

In this fascinating book, with its superb photographs, Gert Chesi, the noted Tyrolean photographer and journalist, presents a lasting record of the traditional life-styles of various African tribes, like the Kirdi, Ashanti, Bororo, Dogon, Peul, Lobi, Somba, Ewe and Karamojong. As an internationally acknowledged contribution to a better understanding of black Africa, the book has already had several printings and has achieved worldwide sales of 90 000 copies in English, French, German, Swedish and Spanish.

Gert Chesi

Voodoo–Africa's Secret Power

276 pages, 128 colour plates, numerous black-and-white photographs. 25 × 30 cm, cloth bound.

After years of work in the field, Gert Chesi presents the first-ever in-depth report on African voodoo. Afro-American syncretism now has a following of over 50 million people throughout the world and the phenomenon continues to attract more and more public attention. This book provides a superb record of the almost unknown African sources of the movement, combining stunning photography with an excellent explanatory text. Published in English, French, German, Swedish and Spanish.

Gert Chesi

Faith Healers in the Philippines

288 pages, 64 colour plates, numerous black-and-white photographs. 25 × 30 cm, cloth bound.

The faith healers of the Philippines have become famous–and controversial–throughout the world, thanks to their 'bloody operations', which in fact are just one aspect of their successful methods of treatment. This book, with its astounding photographs, is the first-ever record of the great variety of methods employed by the Philippine faith healers, whose repertoire is based on shamanistic traditions and biblical sources. In order to present a balanced picture, the author has included interviews with the most famous of the healers, the views of western medical experts, and numerous case studies. Published in English, French and German.

Gert Chesi / Susanne Wenger

A Life with the Gods– In their Yoruba Homeland

256 pages, 76 colour plates, numerous black-and-white photographs. 25 × 30 cm, cloth bound.

The Austrian artist Susanne Wenger has spent the last 30 years living with the Yoruba of Nigeria. Having herself been made a priestess of the tribe, she has worked with native artists to produce a 'New Sacred Art'. In this exciting volume she discusses her life with the gods and describes the deeply rooted cults and religious rituals of the Yoruba. Together with the brilliant photography and commentary by Gert Chesi, this book is an invaluable record of one of the major religious systems of Africa. Published in English and German.

Alexander Orloff

Carnival–Myth and Cult

260 pages, 146 colour plates, numerous black-and-white photographs and illustrations. 25 × 30 cm, cloth bound.

Alexander Orloff, a photographer and journalist of Russian extraction, describes one of the oldest phenomena in the history of mankind, dealing with it in all its variety, from the New Year celebrations of the Ancient Egyptians and Babylonians to the carnival customs of Basle, Binche, Cologne, Nice, Telfs and Viareggio, from the fertility cults of the Greeks and Romans to the carnival fun of Mexico, New Orleans, Haiti, Trinidad and Rio de Janeiro. Published in English, French, German and Spanish.

Perlinger Verlag

A-6300 Wörgl (Austria), Brixentaler Strasse 61, phone (0 53 32) 33 41 / telex 051/205 teltaz